# BUSINESS ETHICS
# AS RATIONAL CHOICE

## John Hooker

*Tepper School of Business*
*Carnegie Mellon University*

**Prentice Hall**

Boston   Columbus   Indianapolis   New York   San Francisco   Upper Saddle River
Amsterdam   Cape Town   Dubai   London   Madrid   Milan   Munich   Paris   Montreal   Toronto
Delhi   Mexico City   Sao Paulo   Sydney   Hong Kong   Seoul   Singapore   Taipei   Tokyo

**Editorial Director:** Sally Yagan
**Editor in Chief:** Eric Svendsen
**Acquisitions Editor:** Kim Norbuta
**Editorial Project Manager:** Claudia Fernandes
**Director of Marketing:** Patrice Lumumba Jones
**Marketing Manager:** Nikki Jones
**Marketing Assistant:** Ian Gold
**Senior Managing Editor:** Judy Leale
**Project Manager:** Debbie Ryan
**Production Manager:** Kathy Sleys
**Design Director:** Jayne Conte
**Cover Designer:** Bruce Kenselaar
**Lead Media Project Manager:** Lisa Rinaldi
**Full-Service Project Management/Composition:** Integra Software Services
**Printer/Binder:** Edwards Brothers, Inc.
**Cover Printer:** Lehigh/Phoenix Color Corp.
**Text Font:** Minion

**Library of Congress Cataloging-in-Publication Data**
Hooker, John
    Business ethics as rational choice / John Hooker.
        p. cm.
    Includes bibliographical references and index.
    ISBN-13: 978-0-13-611867-1 (alk. paper)
    ISBN-10: 0-13-611867-4 (alk. paper)
    1. Business ethics.   2. Decision making—Moral and ethical aspects.   3. Business ethics—Case studies.   I. Title.
    HF5387.H664 2011
    174'.4—dc22

                                                                                2010015500

10 9 8 7 6 5 4 3 2 1

**Prentice Hall**
is an imprint of

www.pearsonhighered.com

ISBN 10:        0-13-611867-4
ISBN 13: 978-0-13-611867-1

# BRIEF CONTENTS

# CONTENTS

# PREFACE

This is a different kind of business ethics book. It focuses on building your decision-making skills, so that you can arrive at, and defend, personal or company decisions in an objective manner that others find convincing. It accomplishes this by bridging the gap between theory and practice, much as an engineering text does. It develops ethical theory with enough rigor and precision to deal with the complexity of real-life situations. It then provides you an opportunity to build expertise through practice—by applying the theory to a wide variety of dilemmas in a disciplined way.

Rather than present full-length case studies or readings, the book succinctly describes 29 business dilemmas, chosen for their realism. It shows how to analyze them by applying specific conditions for ethical conduct derived from the theory. It is based on the premise that an *ethical* choice is at root a *rational* choice, where rationality is understood in a general sense that takes into account the interests of all concerned. The text is accompanied by 106 exercises that gradually develop your analytical skills. The book concludes with an introduction to cross-cultural business ethics.

The book is intended for both professionals and students. It is for those in business or government who desire a conceptual framework and vocabulary that allow them to balance the interests of multiple stakeholders in a fair and convincing fashion. The concise presentation of the basic theory is suitable for busy managers. The case study analyses illustrate the analytical tools at a gradually increasing level of sophistication, so that readers can go as deeply as they wish. New and updated case studies are available online, along with solutions for some of the exercises in the book.

The book is also appropriate for several types of classroom use. It provides the analytical framework for a course in business ethics, where it can be supplemented by full-length case studies or problem-specific articles of interest to the class. It can also form the basis for a short business ethics course or module that is dedicated to skill building. It can provide a common intellectual framework for an ethics-across-the-curriculum program, because faculty in other business areas can digest the compact theoretical treatment with a limited time investment. I have also used this material in executive education programs, where the analytical tools are applied to scenarios supplied by the participants. Finally, ethical analysis provides the perfect occasion to develop argumentative skills in a communication course. An instructor's guide provides suggestions for using the book in these settings as well as solutions for all exercises.

## SUPPLEMENTS

At www.pearsonhighered.com/irc, the following supplements are available to adopting instructors for download. Registration is simple and gives you immediate access to new titles and new editions. If you ever need assistance, our dedicated technical support team is ready to help with the media supplements that accompany this text. Visit http://247.pearsoned.com/ for answers to frequently asked questions and toll-free user support phone numbers.

- Instructor's Manual
- Exercise Solutions

**CourseSmart Textbooks Online** is an exciting new choice for students looking to save money. As an alternative to purchasing the print textbook, students can subscribe to the same content online and save up to 50% off the suggested list price of the print text. With a CourseSmart e-textbook, students can search the text, make notes online, print out reading assignments that incorporate lecture notes, and bookmark important passages for later review. For more information, visit www.coursesmart.com.

## ACKNOWLEDGMENTS

I would like to thank my students and executive workshop participants over the years for providing hundreds of ethical dilemmas, some of which appear here, as well as a laboratory for working out the ideas. I am also indebted to business school colleagues who pointed me to case studies and other materials that are used in their courses and analyzed in this book.

# ABOUT THE AUTHOR

*John Hooker* is T. Jerome Holleran Professor of Business Ethics and Social Responsibility, and Professor of Operations Research, at Carnegie Mellon University. He holds doctoral degrees in philosophy and management science. He teaches at the undergraduate, postgraduate, and professional levels, and he has published over 130 articles and 10 books. He has held visiting posts at universities in several countries, most recently at the London School of Economics. He was head of Carnegie Mellon's undergraduate Business Administration Program, 1996–2001. He reorganized the program, led the design of its curriculum, and received a distinguished service award from the Tepper School for his contributions. In 2009, he received an Award for Sustained Teaching Excellence.

Professor Hooker has equally strong interests in applied mathematics on the one hand and ethics and cross-cultural issues on the other. His books *Integrated Methods for Optimization* and *Logic-Based Methods for Optimization* exemplify the former. He has served on numerous editorial boards and conference program committees related to operations research. He is a Fellow of the Institute for Operations Research and the Management Sciences and a recipient of that institute's Computing Society Award.

His books *Business Ethics as Rational Choice* and *Working Across Cultures* reflect his interests in ethics and cultural matters. He is founding editor-in-chief of the *Journal of Business Ethics Education* and founding director of the Center for International Corporate Responsibility at Carnegie Mellon. He developed the ethics curriculum, including many of the course materials, used in the Tepper School of Business, and he has co-organized four conferences on international corporate responsibility. He has lived and worked in Australia, China, Denmark, India, Qatar, Turkey, the United Kingdom, the United States, and Zimbabwe and has extensive experience in Germany and Mexico. He lives with his wife in his favorite city of Pittsburgh and has one grown-up son. He enjoys attempting to play and compose for the piano.

# Chapter *1*

# Introduction

The title of this book, *Business Ethics as Rational Choice*, may give the impression that I'm going to reduce business ethics to self-interest—that I'm going to say it's rational to be ethical because ethics is good for business.

It is easy to read the title this way because we equate rational behavior with rational self-interest. We believe that any tendency to care about others, to be "moral," must be based on emotion or cultural conditioning, rather than hardheaded reason.

I chose the title to make a point. Rational behavior is much more than rational self-interest. Rationality requires us to consider the interests of others as well as ourselves—not because doing so may eventually serve our own interests, but because neglecting others is inherently illogical and self-contradictory. This may seem hard to believe, but read on.

The book is organized around three specific conditions that a choice of action must meet to be rational and, therefore, to be ethical. These conditions make it possible to put ethical decision making on a reasonably objective basis. When managing a complex organization with multiple stakeholders, you can't rely on gut feeling. You must have a conceptual framework and an ethical vocabulary to defend your decision to others—and to yourself when the going gets tough. Analysis based on rational choice, by its very nature, provides a rational basis for convincing oneself and others.

Rational decision making is a skill, and like any skill, it requires practice. This book is based on the premise that ethics can be learned in much the same way as chemistry or mathematics. It presents the theory and asks you to work through structured exercises until you learn how to apply it. At first, this may not sound like much fun. We like to think of ethics as an area in which we can sit around and exchange opinions, without having to think hard. But a rigorous approach is more satisfying in the long run, because it provides the conceptual equipment necessary to make reasoned and defensible judgments. I think you will come to enjoy the intellectual challenge presented by the exercises.

Because your time is valuable, I kept the expository sections of the book as brief as possible. All of the basic theory appears in Chapters 2 and 3. Merely reading expository material isn't very helpful in any event. You must exercise your cranial muscles by thinking through real cases. Most of the book consists of ethical dilemmas that are analyzed to show how it's done, along with many others left for you to analyze.

An ethics book, no less than ethical theory, must meet the challenge of real-world experience. The materials in this book were developed over several years for the ethics program at the Tepper School of Business at Carnegie Mellon University. The ideas were hammered out in a process of give-and-take with students at undergraduate, MBA, and executive levels, many of whom have little patience for material that doesn't prove convincing and relevant to their careers. Many of the ethical dilemmas in the book were experienced and written up by students and executive workshop participants, and I present them with minimal alteration to ensure realism.

## WHY BUSINESS ETHICS?

Much of the business ethics literature focuses on showing that ethical behavior is good for business. It usually is, but this misses the point of business ethics. Think about it. If ethical behavior were reducible to self-interest, there would be no need for ethics. We could simply figure out how to serve our interests and forget about ethics. Ethics was invented because ethical behavior is not identical with self-interested behavior.

Ethical behavior is closely connected, however, with the welfare of society as a whole. Ethics makes it possible for us to live together. We sometimes lose sight of this fact. We tend to think that the law and the police keep order and that ethics is icing on the cake; that is, it's nice to be ethical, but it's really law enforcement that makes the system work.

This is wrong. It's ethics that makes law enforcement work. Imagine that tomorrow morning all motorists started running red lights. What could the police do about it? Nothing. There are not nearly enough police to monitor thousands of intersections, much less chase down the offenders. Or suppose that tonight people all over town started burglarizing houses and apartments. The police would be powerless to stop it. They can't be everywhere at once. The law is enforceable because there is consensus on what is right and wrong, and most people behave accordingly. The police take care of a few people on the margins who don't get the message.

It is the same in the business world. Laws and regulation are important, but there is too little oversight to enforce them. Repeated waves of business scandals over the last two or three decades demonstrate how easy it is to get away with mischief—perhaps not indefinitely, but long enough to destroy a company. The Western business system works largely because of voluntary compliance.

Even if everyone observes the letter of the law, it's easy enough to violate its spirit. The financial sector alone amply illustrates how clever operators can find loopholes or stay a step ahead of the regulators, resulting in mayhem. But what does it mean to obey the spirit of the law? It means to abide voluntarily by the ethical principles that underlie the law.

If ethics is to do its job, society must inculcate a disposition to be ethical. We must (a) agree on what is ethical and (b) act accordingly. Every culture has mechanisms to accomplish both. In Western cultures, part (a) is largely accomplished by building rational consensus. We *talk the talk* as well as *walk the walk*. We come to understand why it makes sense to obey traffic laws and respect property. We may break the speed limit, but perhaps it's because we haven't convinced each other that we should drive more slowly.

This process of building rational consensus is particularly important in complex business organizations, where there are many stakeholders with reasonable but conflicting claims. Gone are the days when a business manager could simply maximize the bottom line, if they ever existed. There is a growing realization that business decisions are inextricably linked with society at large. The platitudes we learned in kindergarten aren't going to work here. We require a sophisticated discourse that can arrive at equitable and convincing solutions. We have developed advanced methods for finance, operations, and marketing. It is time we did the same for ethics.

This is where business ethics comes into the picture. Its task is to provide a conceptual framework for making defensible business decisions that consider all stakeholders. Fortunately,

Western civilization provides us a rich tradition to draw from. Intelligent people have been developing a rational basis for Western ethics ever since Socrates.

A central task of this book is to work out a rational reconstruction of this intellectual tradition that makes sense to us today and that has the power and subtlety to deal with complex issues. The theory is not as precise or well developed as chemistry and mathematics, but there are two good reasons for this. One is that ethics is harder than chemistry and even mathematics (I know, because I am a mathematician). The other is that far more effort has been invested in the rigorous study of chemistry and mathematics than in the rigorous development of ethics.

You can help remedy this deficit. By working through this material and applying it at work and in life, you can do your part to bring ethical reasoning out of kindergarten and into the adult world.

## DISPELLING THE MYTHS

My experience indicates that a few popular myths tend to block us from making the kind of progress in ethics that we have made in other fields. Let's take them one at a time.

- *Myth 1. We learn ethics as little kids. When we reach adulthood, it is too late to change our behavior.*

Early childhood is important in character development, but decades of research in developmental psychology show that ethical maturity grows with cognitive ability.[1] As we develop the capacity to think through our actions, our behavior tends to become more ethical. Obviously there are exceptions, but they are exceptions, not the rule. Cognitive ability, in turn, can grow throughout life, right up into old age. Some writers in moral development suggest that the highest stage of moral development is reached only in the 60s or later, if ever.[2] Training in ethical analysis is one way to move this process along, while providing skills that relate directly to decision making.

- *Myth 2. There is no point in studying ethics, because we all know what's right. It's just a matter of doing it.*

Then why do we disagree all the time? My students and workshop participants differ on every ethical issue I present to them. If we disagree, we can't all be correct. Certainly, doing what is right can be hard even when we know what is right, but often we don't know.

I grant that there is a good deal of consensus on basic matters of right and wrong. Otherwise, society would have fallen apart long ago, as I have already mentioned. But there is a pressing need for greater consensus, particularly on complex issues that require careful analysis, some of which may determine the fate of our civilization.

- *Myth 3. Business ethics is simple. Just don't do anything you wouldn't want to appear on the front page of the newspaper, or you wouldn't want your mother to know about.*

This one is surprisingly popular, even though it stands up to scrutiny about ten seconds. Suppose you lay off a thousand workers. Some of them become alcoholics, beat their spouses and children, and become physically ill or clinically depressed (all regular consequences of layoffs). The local economy is decimated, crime soars, and lives are ruined. You wouldn't want this to appear on the front page of the newspaper, or on the back page, for that matter. There is a good chance your mother wouldn't approve, either. Nonetheless, it may have been the only ethical choice in a difficult situation. The alternatives may have been even worse.

- *Myth 4. There is no point in analyzing ethical issues, because ethics is just a matter of opinion. I have my view and you have yours, and that's the end of it.*

Try to remember this the next time you are mugged. Pardon my sarcasm, but it's hard for me to accept that anyone really believes this.

- *Myth 5. Studying ethics will have no effect, because human beings are motivated only by self-interest, not ethical theories. We learned this long ago from Adam Smith, who observed that self-interest drives the market system and makes it work to our benefit, as if guided by an invisible hand.*

Adam Smith said no such thing. The very first sentence of his book *Theory of Moral Sentiments*[3] states that human beings are motivated by concern for others as well as themselves, and the rest of the book makes an extended case for this proposition. His second book, *The Wealth of Nations*,[4] describes the central role of self-interest in a market economy and uses the image of an invisible hand. Yet most of the book deals with ways that self-interest also undermines a market system and how this might be prevented. Smith saw government regulation as a major part of the solution, and after finishing the book, he spent the rest of his working life as a regulator.

Of course, whatever Smith said, he may have been wrong. Yet recent research in fields ranging from neuropsychology to genetics tends to confirm his view that altruism plays an important role in human behavior. Business ethics can refine and reinforce the human tendency to care about others by placing it on a rational basis that is practical and convincing in a business environment.

## HOW TO USE THIS BOOK

The first step is to read Chapters 2 and 3, which contain the basic concepts. Think critically about the ideas as you go along. If you disagree with them, then so much the better, because you can try to reconstruct the theory in a way that makes sense to you. This is a good way to start the mental calisthenics that build decision-making skills. These chapters also provide exercises that verify and deepen your understanding.

The next step is to work through the case studies in Chapter 4. These are chosen to draw out key implications of the conditions for rational choice and show them in action. The analyses are kept to a simple level, and they are sometimes incomplete, because you are just getting started. The exercises in the body of the chapter help you think about the analyses, and those at the end present some dilemmas for you to analyze on your own.

Chapter 5 analyzes dilemmas experienced at the individual level by my MBA students, and Chapter 6 moves to more complex case studies that relate to company policy. I suggest beginning with the cases that interest you most. It is good practice to analyze a case on your own and then compare your thinking with the analysis in the text. Both chapters present a number of additional scenarios for you to analyze as exercises.

It is helpful to discuss these cases with your colleagues or classmates, because this affords practice in articulating your arguments. A structured debate is also a useful activity. The case analyses, particularly the longer ones in Chapter 6, are most instructive after you have immersed yourself in the issue. When you disagree with the conclusions of an analysis, you should pinpoint the spot where you believe the argument goes astray and reconstruct it as needed.

When working through exercises, it is essential that you don't simply state your views, or present some arguments that sound reasonable to you. You should specifically apply the conditions for rational choice.

You may be concerned about whether you arrive at the right answer for an exercise, or if there is in fact a right answer. The key point is that you apply the conditions of rational choice in a cogent manner, following the pattern of the analyses in the chapter. Even then, you may arrive at a different conclusion than someone else for several reasons. The exercise may not provide enough factual detail to resolve the issue, in which case you might want to analyze the issue based on two or more factual scenarios. An important part of the analysis is determining which facts matter. Or the issue may be too hard to resolve satisfactorily without advanced skills, in which case you can still make some progress by ruling out certain alternatives. Finally, the state of the art in ethical reasoning may be inadequate to draw definitive conclusions.

This state of affairs may seem discouraging, but it is no different in other fields. If an engineering text asks you to design a truss bridge over a certain ravine, there may be more than one solution. A professional engineer is likely to recognize additional factors that students overlook. Even the most experienced practitioners may disagree over some aspects of the design. This doesn't mean that there is no objectivity in engineering. One can still distinguish good solutions from bad solutions, and it is the same in ethics.

A rationality-based approach may seem to reduce ethics to logic chopping, ignoring the subtlety and ambiguity of real life. This is by no means the intent. Judgment and experience are as important as close reasoning, and good decisions come from the heart as well as the mind. Again, this is true of any applied field. Designing a transit system or a hospital involves much more than solving equations. Nonetheless, it is essential to know the basics. Wisdom is built on a foundation of rigorous analysis and clear thinking. This text shows how to "solve the equations" in ethics. You take it from there.

The final chapter is a brief introduction to cross-cultural ethics. It moves beyond the rationality-based framework of Western ethics to provide a glimpse of some of the radically different ethical traditions developed by other cultures. To maintain the practical bent of the book, it exemplifies these normative systems with a series of real-life case studies of corruption. The aim is partly to alert you to the necessity of learning about other cultures when doing business in them. An equally important objective, however, is to put Western ethics into perspective, clarifying its assumptions and highlighting its strengths and weaknesses.

## Notes

1. See for example: W. G. Perry, *Intellectual and Ethical Development in the College Years*, New York: Holt, 1968; L. Kohlberg, *The Philosophy of Moral Development: Moral Stages and the Idea of Justice*, New York: Harper & Row, 1981; R. Kegan, *The Evolving Self: Meaning and Process in Human Development*, Cambridge, MA: Harvard University Press, 1981; J. W. Fowler, *Stages of Faith: The Psychology of Human Development and the Quest for Meaning*, New York: Harper & Row, 1982; S. D. Parks, "Is it too late? Young adults and the formation of professional ethics," in T. R. Piper, M. C. Gentile and S. D. Parks, eds., *Can Ethics Be Taught? Perspectives, Challenges and Approaches at Harvard Business School*, Cambridge, MA: Harvard University Press, 1993; M. L. Hoffman, *Empathy and Moral Development: Implications for Caring and Justice*, Cambridge, UK: Cambridge University Press, 2000; J. C. Gibbs, *Moral Development and Reality: Beyond the Theories of Kohlberg and Hoffman*, Thousand Oaks, CA: Sage Publications, 2003.

2. For example, see Kohlberg, *The Philosophy of Moral Development*; Fowler, *Stages of Faith*.

3. 1759, last revision 1790.

4. *Inquiry into the Nature and Causes of the Wealth of Nations*, 1776, last revision 1789.

# Chapter 2

# Conditions for Rational Choice

This chapter presents three specific conditions that any rational decision must satisfy. Briefly, they are:

- *The generalization test.* A rational choice must be generalizable.
- *The utilitarian test.* A rational choice must maximize utility, subject to the other conditions for rationality.
- *The virtue test.* A rational choice must be consistent with who you are and why you are here.

I will explain these shortly, but it is important to recognize that no explanation can fully convey their meaning. They can be understood only in application. Properly applying the conditions is a sophisticated skill that is developed with diligent practice. The rest of this book provides many opportunities to practice, and life provides many more.

## JENNIFER'S CHOICE

Let's begin with an ethical dilemma that will serve as a running example as we discuss the conditions for rational choice. It is fictitious but similar to situations that business students frequently encounter.

While interviewing for jobs, MBA student Jennifer learned about a very attractive opening at Glamour Finance in New York City. It matched her interests and abilities perfectly. She interviewed on site, and everyone expressed enthusiasm about her potential for helping clients to realize their business goals. Shortly after the interview, however, Glamour announced a hiring freeze, due to a global financial crisis. The freeze dragged on through much of the spring semester, and Jennifer's contacts at Glamour could not predict when it would be lifted.

In the meantime, Jennifer received two reasonably good offers from firms with which she had interviewed before going to New York City. She tried to keep her options open, but graduation was near, and her classmates were talking about the great job offers they had accepted. Her parents were asking about her prospects. Her best friend Heather urged her to get real and accept a job. Finally, when her offers were about to expire, she signed with Midwest Consulting, which is based in a small city.

About a week later, Jennifer received a call from Glamour announcing that the firm was hiring again. Her employment contract was ready to sign. Distraught, she told Heather about her rotten luck. Heather's reply was, "What's the problem? Just tell Midwest that an unexpected opportunity came up. Employers understand that these things happen."

I have conducted a number of discussions of this dilemma. People cite a variety of reasons why Jennifer should accept the New York job: Midwest will have no problem finding someone else, Jennifer will be happier doing a job she likes, there is probably an escape clause in the employment contract, employers sometimes renege on job offers and should expect the same from employees, and so forth. However, others point out that Jennifer made a promise, a contract is a contract, she cannot expect employers to play fair with her if she does not play fair with them, the opposing arguments just rationalize self-interested behavior, and so forth. Generally people walk out of the room with the views they initially expressed, and we get nowhere toward resolving the issue. So it goes with most ethical dilemmas.

The problem is that people talk past each other, exchanging arguments that seem to convince only those who already agree with the conclusion. There is no rational convergence, and people tend to lose faith in the ability of reason to resolve such disputes. Our approach in this book will be to avoid advancing arguments merely because they sound reasonable, but to discipline ourselves to apply only the conditions of rational choice. This will allow us to make some progress toward resolving the issue.

However, you must be patient. No resolution of Jennifer's dilemma will be possible until all three conditions mentioned at the beginning of the chapter have been introduced, and even then the analysis will be incomplete. One can't do triple integration on the first day of calculus class, and it is the same in ethics. But considering that most ethical debates get nowhere, even modest progress toward resolution should be a welcome departure from the norm.

## THE GENERALIZATION TEST

The conditions for rational choice are based on a simple premise: There must be a reason behind every action. I will defend this premise shortly, but first I want to derive the generalization test from it.

### The Basic Argument

If I have a reason for my action, then the reason *justifies* the action for me. This is what reasons do: They justify the actions for which they are reasons. Yet if a reason justifies an action for me, then it justifies the action for anyone. Either the reason justifies the action or it doesn't. If it does, then it justifies the action for anyone to whom it applies.

For example, suppose I notice a display of wristwatches in a shop. They are not protected under glass but are readily available for the taking. No clerks or security personnel are in the vicinity, and there are no surveillance cameras. I could easily pocket one of these and stroll out of the shop. Let's suppose that I decide to steal one of the watches because I can easily get away with it. Then I am committed to saying that anyone who can easily get away with stealing a watch should do so. If ease of theft justifies stealing, then it justifies stealing.

I may protest that this reason doesn't work for everyone, because not everyone cares to have a new watch. Then I actually have two reasons for stealing the watch: I can get a free watch without risk of being caught, and I would like to have a new watch. To be consistent, I must say that theft is justified for anyone who wants a new watch and can easily get away with stealing one. When I choose to steal for these reasons, I am choosing theft for anyone who has the same reasons to steal.

But now I am caught in inconsistency. I have adopted a policy of theft for everyone who wants a new watch and can easily get away with stealing one. But if all such people were to steal watches, it would no longer be easy to steal the watch and get away with it. The shop owner would have discovered that most customers are thieves and would secure watches in a locked case. The only reason I can steal is that others are honest enough not to do the same. I therefore don't choose for others to steal watches after all, because this would frustrate my own purposes. I am inconsistent: By choosing to steal, I choose theft for others who have my reasons to steal, and yet my reasons presuppose that they don't steal.

Stealing the watch fails the *generalization test*, which can be phrased as follows:

- *Generalization test. The reasons for my action should be consistent with the assumption that everyone who has the same reasons acts the same way.*

I am not saying that everyone with the same reasons *would* steal a watch if I did. I am making no prediction about what other people would do. I am only observing that *if* they *all* followed my example, the reasons for my own theft would no longer apply. This is enough to show inconsistency. Nor am I saying simply that I wouldn't *want* others to steal watches. This is not enough to establish inconsistency in my reasons for stealing. The specific test is whether my reasons for stealing would still apply if all others with the same reasons to steal did so. They would not.

To take another example, let's suppose that a student is tempted to cheat on an exam because it will improve his grade and career prospects. To apply the generalization test, imagine that students cheated whenever these same reasons apply (i.e., practically anytime they take an exam). Grades would be practically meaningless, because nearly everyone would make all As. Cheating would no longer improve the student's career prospects. The student's reasons for cheating are therefore inconsistent with the assumption that others who have the same reasons to cheat do so. Cheating for these reasons fails the generalization test and is therefore irrational and unethical.

## Corollaries of the Generalization Test

The cheating example suggests a restatement of the generalization test that is less precise but sometimes helpful:

- *Corollary 1. An action is unethical if its general adoption would undermine a practice it presupposes.*

Cheating fails this test because it undermines the practice of grading. This is not actually a restatement of the generalization test but a *corollary*, or a more specific form of the test that an action must pass if it is to pass the original test. Yet an action that passes a corollary may fail the original test.

For example, suppose I build a cabin in a Deep Green Forest because I can afford to do so, I want to live in an unspoiled area, and I particularly like Deep Green Forest. Let's suppose further that if everyone satisfying these conditions built a cabin, the cabins would spoil the forest. My action does not undermine a practice that it presupposes, in any clear sense, and so it passes Corollary 1. But it clearly fails the generalization test.

Another corollary of the generalization test is the *free rider* principle, which is again vague but sometimes helpful:

- *Corollary 2. One shouldn't be a free rider on the efforts of others.*

A literal case of free riding occurs in some European countries where public transit passengers are normally not asked to show their tickets. Riding without a ticket is unethical because it presupposes that others who have similar reasons to ride for free nonetheless buy a ticket. If they didn't buy tickets, it would be impossible for anyone to ride for free.

A third corollary is particularly useful. It applies when I have two types of reasons for my action: the circumstances are right to perform the action and the action achieves the desired purpose. For example, I build the wilderness cabin when the circumstances are right (I can afford it, I want to live in an unspoiled area, and I particularly like Deep Green Forest), and I can achieve a certain purpose by performing the act (live in an unspoiled area). Let's say that an action is *generalized* when everyone for whom the circumstances are right performs the act. Then the generalization test implies the following:

- *Corollary 3. An action is unethical if generalizing the action is inconsistent with achieving its purpose.*

Thus if my action of building a cabin is generalized, it would be impossible for those who move into cabins to achieve the purpose of the action. The action fails Corollary 3 and therefore the generalization test.

A subtle point arises when generalizing an action is consistent with its reasons in a particular case but not in general. Suppose I build a cabin in a corner of Deep Green Forest that happens to be almost completely surrounded by a national park, where no one can build cabins. If everyone with my reasons for building a cabin in Deep Green Forest did so, the reasons would still apply in my case. I would still live in an unspoiled area, thanks to the national park, even though everyone else in the forest would lose this benefit. (The fact that my cabin is in the corner of the forest is not one of my reasons for building it. It is enough that the cabin be secluded.) My action is nonetheless ungeneralizable because it is impossible for *everyone* to enjoy seclusion if everyone with these reasons built a cabin.

- *Corollary 4. An action is unethical if generalizing the action is inconsistent with the possibility that everyone who performs the action achieves its purpose.*

## Why Acts Must Have Reasons

This whole affair is based on the premise that acts are based on reasons that are taken to justify the action. The source of this premise is a deeply held Western tradition that free agents are *rational* agents and therefore act for a reason. This allows us to distinguish free action from mere behavior, even if we subscribe to a scientific worldview that sees all of our actions as the inevitable result of physical causes.

If a mosquito bites me, this is mere behavior. I don't judge the mosquito morally, because it didn't "freely choose" to bite. The bite was merely the result of chemical reactions in the mosquito's body. Human actions can also be given a causal explanation of this kind, but they can be explained in a second way: by talking about the agent's reasons. It makes no sense to say that the mosquito bit because she thought to herself, "I'm going to bite that human because I'm hungry and I think I can get away before I get swatted." However, it is often very reasonable to explain human actions by attributing reasons to the agent. The action is explained as the outcome of rational deliberation as well as the result of physical causes.

The behavior of computers and robots may someday be more easily explained as the result of the machine's own deliberation than as the outcome of an algorithm. This would make machines moral agents that are bound by ethical obligation, no less than humans.

When the reasons for an action are inconsistent, as when they fail the generalization test, they are not reasons. Inconsistent reasons cannot explain behavior. An action taken for inconsistent reasons is therefore not really an action, but mere behavior. It is like the mosquito's bite, which can be given only a causal explanation. This is why I assume that there must be a reason behind every action.

This is not to say that we humans never conduct ourselves unthinkingly or from habit. We do all the time, and probably must, because constant decision making would be unbearable. But we also choose to cultivate habits or allow them to continue, and we are ethically responsible for these choices.

## Identifying the Reasons for an Action

If the generalization test is to apply to the reasons for an action, then we must identify what the reasons are. Ultimately, the reasons are what we choose them to be, but it is important to identify what we have chosen.

The basic rule is that the reasons must be necessary and sufficient for the action. Each reason must be *necessary* in the sense that if it did not apply, I would not perform the action. Thus I would not steal a watch if either of my reasons for doing so were absent—if it were not easy to get away with it or if I had no desire for a new watch.

The reasons as a group must also be *sufficient* in the sense that I would be willing to perform the act whenever they all apply. If I would steal a watch whenever I wanted a new one and could get away with the crime, then these reasons are sufficient for the theft. If I would not, there must be other reasons I am stealing it.

The necessity criterion prevents us from framing our reasons so narrowly that every action is generalizable. For example, Gertrude Grosvenor might insist that she stole a watch because she wanted one, she could easily get away with it, and her name is Gertrude Grosvenor. She protests that her reasons are generalizable, because she could just as easily get away with stealing the watch if all the Gertrude Grosvenors of the world stole watches.

This is the problem of *scope*. Gertrude passed the generalization test by drawing the scope of her action too narrowly. Her name has nothing to do with whether she steals. If it did, then she would stop stealing the moment she discovers a birth certificate in her mother's attic showing that her real name is Genevieve Grosvenor. But she wouldn't stop stealing on this account. Her name is not one of her reasons for stealing.

In general, the scope of an action is the set of circumstances under which it would be performed. The scope is too narrow when unnecessary reasons are cited, and it is too broad when some necessary reasons are left out. The adjustment of scope will often prove to be a subtle and difficult aspect of judging an act. But if an ethical theory were not subtle it would be inadequate for the complex situations life presents us.

## Jennifer's Choice

Recall that Jennifer faces a decision as to whether to break her employment contract with Midwest Consulting, so she can accept a more attractive offer at Glamour Finance. Let's check whether taking this act passes the generalization test. To do so, we must identify the reasons for her choice. The most obvious reason is that she prefers an employment contract with Glamour.

Breaking an employment contract to get a better one is not generalizable. If students broke their employment contracts whenever they got a better offer, companies would not bother with contracts that promise employment in the first place. The whole point of promising employment is that, in return, the company can rest assured that the student's job search is over and will work for them. If Jennifer's action were generalized, she wouldn't be able to get the contract she wants with Glamour, because Glamour would not be issuing contracts that promise employment. This makes the breach of contract ungeneralizable and unethical.

We can say something stronger. Jennifer's breach of contract would be unethical even if she had no desire to contract with another firm, but simply found it convenient to break the agreement.

By definition, Jennifer cannot break an employment contract without having made the contract. Breaking the contract is therefore ethical only if making *and* breaking the contract is an ethical act. But making a contract and then breaking it simply for convenience is not generalizable. It would be impossible to make an employment contract in the first place if everyone broke contracts whenever it is convenient to do so.

Jennifer may protest that I have drawn the scope too broadly, because her reasons are more complex than I have made out. She acted in good faith all along. The offer from Glamour was unexpected, and she didn't interview after signing with Midwest. These are all part of her reasons. Making exceptions in such cases may be consistent with the practices that make employment contracts possible.

Yet on reflection, this, too, fails the generalization test. Imagine what it would be like if students were always willing to accept an unsolicited offer after signing a contract for a less-attractive job. Companies would keep making them offers in the hope of luring them away from the jobs they had accepted. Again, the employment contract would not mean that the job search is over, and companies would have no reason to offer contracts that promise employment.

It would be like an auction at which the auctioneer keeps accepting bids after shouting "sold." The bidding would never be over. Auctions would be impossible, because people would never know when they have bought the merchandise.

There may be another way for Jennifer to escape from her commitment to Midwest. Employment contracts often have some kind of escape clause for both parties. In fact, contracts frequently do not actually promise employment, but only the salary and other terms as long as the employment lasts. Conversely, the employee may have the option of resigning at any time without penalty, perhaps after giving notice, such as two weeks. Jennifer might therefore decide to give notice even though she has not started work.

Let's grant that this maneuver is legal. The difficulty is, from an ethical point of view, she promised more than this. Everyone recognizes that a change in life circumstances may require a change of job, such as marriage, children, or unexpected financial problems. Or after working at a company for a while, one may be ready to move on to another position. In such cases, giving notice is reasonable and expected. But barring unforeseen circumstances, Jennifer promised to work for Midwest *for the time being*. Again, the whole point of signing with Midwest is to indicate that Jennifer has made up her mind where to work, whatever may be the technical terms of the contract. Similarly, the whole point of Midwest's offering a job to Jennifer is to indicate that the company has made up its mind whom to hire, whatever "employment at will" language may appear in the contract. Midwest is promising to employ her *for the time being*, unless there is an unexpected change of circumstances, such as company bankruptcy or Jennifer's failure to perform satisfactorily. Companies sometimes renege on their promise, but this doesn't make it right to do so, or show that it is permissible for Jennifer to renege.

This analysis does not tell Jennifer precisely how long she must work for Midwest to honor her agreement or how long the company must employ her. But it at least tells her that the two-week notice maneuver is unacceptable.

The whole situation changes, of course, if Midwest releases Jennifer from the contract. She might go to Midwest to explain the situation and learn that the company has found another MBA student whom they would actually prefer to hire. Jennifer and the company therefore agree to forget about their employment contract. This is clearly generalizable, because the practice of employment contracts is not undermined if they are abrogated only with mutual consent.

The consent must be genuine, however. If Midwest releases Jennifer from the contract only because they see that they are going to lose her anyway, this is not consent. From an ethical point of view, Jennifer is in breach of her promise to work for Midwest, whatever may be its legal status.

As a last resort, Jennifer might concede that breaking her contract is problematic but insist that the circumstances justify it. At Midwest she would be bored and unmotivated, while at Glamour she will be enthusiastic and much more likely to keep customers happy. Midwest can easily find someone else qualified for their job, while she is uniquely suited to the Glamour job. Can these considerations override the generalization test? Or to put it differently, can the end justify the means? I will deal with this issue shortly, when I discuss the second condition for rational choice.

### Judging Generalizability

The generalization test requires that we judge the consequences of generalizing an action. This raises the question of how we can really know what the consequences of a generalized action would be. For example, Jennifer may ask how she can be sure that companies would keep making offers if students would accept them. Fortunately, it is not necessarily to *know* the consequences of generalizing an action. It is only necessary to be consistent in one's beliefs. The generalization test, like all the rationality tests, is a test for logical consistency.

Thus if Jennifer's beliefs about how the world works imply that she would be unable to make and break an employment contract if all students did so, then her action fails the generalization test. Similarly, if my beliefs about the world imply that the shop would lock up its watches if customers regularly stole them, then my theft is not generalizable. The generalization test can therefore be more precisely stated.

- *Generalization test (refined). The reason for my action should be consistent, based on my understanding of how the world works, with the assumption that everyone who has the same reason will act the same way.*

Suppose, however, Jennifer refuses to acknowledge that employers would continue to make offers if students accepted them after signing. Then she may claim that her beliefs about employer behavior are consistent with the possibility of generalizing her actions. In this case we must ask whether her refusal is reasonable, given her experience and her other beliefs about the world. If not, no rational reconstruction can be given for the thinking behind her behavior. This means that breaking the contract is not an action, and therefore not an ethical action. To be ethical, she need not be *right* about whether employers would continue to make offers, but only *rational* in her beliefs about it.

### Professional Ethics

A central issue for business ethics is how to understand professional ethics, which sometimes seems to impose obligations that conflict with ethics in a broader sense. A business executive, for example, may be professionally bound to lay off workers, or pollute the environment within legal limits, for the sake of profits—even when this hurts people. Similar dilemmas arise in other professions. A physician may be professionally obligated to withhold a cancer drug from patients because it has not been governmentally approved, even when it could save lives.

The generalization test plays a central role in analyzing professional obligation. To see why, it is helpful to think about why we have professions. They assure the public that it can expect a certain standard of conduct from members of the profession. Professional standards relieve patients of the burden of investigating the background of every physician who might treat them, or businesses the burden of administering a CPA examination to every accountant they hire.

This is not only socially efficient but holds every member of the profession to a promise. An individual who walks into an examination room wearing a long, white coat and displays medical diplomas on the wall makes a promise to the patient waiting there. She promises to conform to the standard of conduct that the medical professional has led the public to expect. Accountants who write "CPA" after their name promise to adhere to generally accepted accounting practices. Because the duty to keep a promise is grounded in the generalization principle, it typically plays a prominent role in the analysis of professional obligation.

Settling issues of professional obligation actually has two components. One is an empirical matter of determining what the profession has in fact led its clients to expect. Exactly what does the business executive promise stockholders, and what does the physician promise patients? The other is the ethical matter of when there is an obligation to keep these promises, particularly when doing so can cause harm. This is an issue that arises with promise keeping in general and can be treated with the same type of analysis. Even in everyday nonprofessional life, we sometimes find that our promises conflict with other obligations and must decide what to do about it.

Professional ethics is therefore not a different kind of ethics that may be at odds with general ethics. It is a particular kind of promise-keeping obligation that is considered along with the other elements of a case and evaluated with the same conditions for rational choice. This means that we can't make blanket statements about what professional obligation requires. We can't say that an executive's fiduciary obligation to owners always requires profit maximization within the law, or that a physician must always go by the book. It depends on the particulars of the case.

## Fiduciary Duty to Stockholders

Fiduciary duty requires closer examination, because it is frequently cited as justification for taking whatever action may be necessary to maximize profit. "Fiduciary" literally means loyalty, and fiduciary duty is normally interpreted as a duty to be loyal to stockholders by advancing their financial interests. This most closely describes the position of board members and senior executives, as opposed to middle managers and other employees. When someone joins the board of directors or signs on as CEO, there is at least an implicit promise to represent the financial interests of the owners.

The first point to recognize is that the owners are ultimately responsible for the actions of the firm. If the firm shuts down a plant and moves its operations to a low-wage country, for the sake of profitability, the owners are responsible for this decision. If it is unethical, the owners are unethical. So the fundamental and prior question always is, is the action in question an ethical choice for the owners? If so, then board members and executives carry it out on their behalf in good conscience. If not, we must ask whether the directors and top executives of the firm are nonetheless obligated to carry out the action to keep their fiduciary promise.

As with professional obligation in general, this is a promise-keeping issue that must be resolved one case at a time. We might anticipate, however, that only in fairly unusual situations is one obligated to act on behalf of someone for whom the action would be unethical. The directors have specific duties that are mandated by the corporate charter or by law, but the law rarely requires strict profit maximization, as is often supposed in the popular imagination. The key point is this: The mere fact that an action maximizes profit does not establish a fiduciary obligation to carry it out, particularly if it is unethical for the owners. Further argument is required.

The situation is different with employees other than top executives. Their duties to the firm derive from their employee contracts, instructions from superiors, and the expectations associated with their specific positions. Fiduciary obligation is not directly relevant, except to the extent that their specific duties tend to enhance profitability. In fact, if superiors instructed them to take actions that reduce profitability, they would normally be obligated to do so. The common defense that "I must do this because I have a fiduciary duty to maximize profits" is therefore invalid for employees other than the most senior executives.

## Exercises

1. Give a simple argument that breaking a promise, simply because it is convenient to do so, fails the generalization test. Note that one can break a promise only if it is possible to make a promise.
2. Give a simple argument that lying, merely for convenience, fails the generalization test. Assume that the lie would achieve its purpose only if it is believed.
3. As an ambulance driver, you normally use a siren and flashing lights only for an emergency. At the moment you are driving the vehicle to an important meeting with your boss that may determine whether you will be laid off due to budget cuts. You lingered a bit too long at lunch before departing and therefore turn on the siren so that you can arrive on time. Suppose for the sake of argument that this is legal. Is it generalizable?
4. The situation is the same as in the previous exercise, except that you are running late because of a very unusual traffic jam on the route. You can still arrive on time by using the siren. Is this generalizable? What exactly is the scope in this case? *Hint*: If you are willing to use the siren due to a traffic delay, would you be willing to use it for other kinds of delay? Why not?
5. While walking down Fifth Avenue in New York City, you see a $100 bill on the pavement. You take the money and spend it because you have no way of knowing who dropped it. This is legal, but is it generalizable?
6. You shop at a grocery that arranges milk bottles so that the oldest ones are in front and the freshest in the rear. You reach behind the older bottles to select the one at the very back. Your reason for doing so is to obtain the freshest milk. Does your behavior pass the generalization test?
7. As you are about to board an aircraft, it is announced that the plane will be boarded by zones to expedite the process. However, you would like to board before your zone is called to make sure you can find space for your carry-on luggage in an overhead compartment. Is this generalizable?
8. While commuting home from work, you take a detour through a residential area to avoid a congested main artery. Because only a few drivers take the detour, it removes several minutes from your commuting time due to the light traffic. Is your action generalizable?
9. In the previous exercise, suppose that a few commuters can drive through the residential area unnoticed, but if many cars used the detour, the traffic would become a noisy and hazardous nuisance in the neighborhood. Does this have a bearing on the generalizability of your action?
10. In Exercise 8, suppose that you are taking the detour only because few people know the city as well as you do. If many people knew about the detour and were nonetheless avoiding it, you would follow their example. Is your action generalizable?
11. *Music shop temptation.* While browsing in a music shop, you spot a CD recording of Arnold Schönberg's *Pierrot Lunaire*. You love this piece, but you are absolutely certain that no one else within a thousand-mile radius can bear listening to this abstract atonal music. The shop is lax about security, and you can easily walk out with the CD without being noticed. You conclude that stealing the CD, because of your unique affection for what others regard as incomprehensible noise, is generalizable. Are you right?
12. Police have closed one lane of a highway due to an accident. A long queue of traffic has formed in the lane that remains open, because drivers slow down to view the accident. However, a few drivers bypass the queue by driving along another lane up to the point of closure and then rely on polite drivers to let them merge at the front of the queue. Is this behavior generalizable? Assume it is legal.
13. In the previous exercise, is it generalizable for a driver at the front of the queue to allow someone to merge? Assume it is legal.
14. You decide to play in an amateur tennis tournament because you know you are the best player in town and will certainly win the trophy and prize money. This is the only reason you are playing the tournament. Is your decision to play in the tournament generalizable? If not, under what sort of rationale would your entry in the tournament be generalizable?
15. You are considering whether your cable TV business should enter the market in Anywheresville, which presently has no cable service. You expect a few other cable companies will do the same. However, past experience in towns of this size shows that only one cable provider will survive. Your only reason for entering the competition is to drive the other companies out. Is a decision to enter this market generalizable?

16. *Damage expense.*[1] Chris is a new hire at a manufacturing company, which pays his moving expenses. However, the movers seriously damage an expensive piece of furniture. The insurance covers only a small fraction of the cost. Chris mentions this to his boss Bob, who tells him to cover it by padding his expense account over the next few months. Chris is surprised by this suggestion, because in their previous conversations, Bob has impressed him as having a high sense of business ethics. (a) Is it generalizable for Chris to pad the expense reports? Be sure to state the scope clearly. (b) Suppose coworkers tell Chris that this kind of padding goes on all the time at the company. Does this change the analysis?

17. *Upgrading the refinery.* You are plant manager at a refinery that meets all environmental regulations. However, the mayor of a nearby community is pressuring you to install new technology that would reduce emissions below mandated levels. You respond that your plant is more cost-efficient than some of your competitors because they bore the cost of installing the new technology. Putting the equipment in your plant would erase this advantage and perhaps result in a plant shutdown. However, the mayor, who has taken a course in Ethics as Rational Choice, points out that your rationale is not generalizable. If all plants followed your example, then keeping the old technology would no longer make your plant the most cost-efficient. How should you respond?

18. Ordinarily, an action that fails the generalization test would continue to fail if the scope were broadened. This is because a rationale is less likely to be generalizable when it applies to more people. However, there are exceptions. Can you think of one?

## THE UTILITARIAN TEST

The reasons for our actions often have a means–ends structure. You may attend class in order to improve your grade, but the grade is itself a means to a degree, which perhaps is a means to a better job, which is itself a means to acquiring happiness, serving others, or whatever. At some point, this regress must reach an *end* or ultimate purpose, or perhaps several ends, if it is to justify any of your actions as means.

We obviously cannot justify our actions in this way unless we get straight on what our ends are. Once we do that, to be rational, we must choose actions that are means to these ends, rather than means to something else or to nothing in particular. We often fail to meet even this simple condition, particularly in the business world. It is easy to get caught up in the struggle of competition and forget what it is all for. Yet we cannot decide how much to sacrifice to maximize stock price until we have determined what we are ultimately trying to accomplish. Almost certainly, a high stock price is not an end in itself, because we wouldn't care about it unless it were necessary to achieve some further end. To be rational, we must identify this end.

### Maximizing Utility

*Utilitarianism*, in its simplest form, suggests that we have or should have some ultimate end that might be called *utility*. This could be pleasure, happiness, or whatever you prefer. High grades, a good job, and a big salary are instrumentally good, while pleasure and happiness are perhaps inherently good. Rationality requires us to decide what is inherently good and aim for it consistently.

We can take this a step further, and this is a crucial step. Suppose I regard happiness as inherently good, my ultimate goal. If creating happiness justifies an action, then creating *anyone's* happiness justifies the action. Otherwise it is not happiness, in and of itself, that justifies the action, as we are supposing. This means that if I can do something to make people happier, I will want to do it. Otherwise I don't really believe happiness is inherently good! I must, in some sense, maximize utility across the whole population, or as the traditional formula goes, achieve the greatest good for the greatest number.

I may protest that *my* happiness is inherently good, not just anyone's. It is my happiness that justifies my action, not happiness in general. But to be rational in distinguishing my happiness from someone else's, there must be some difference that justifies the distinction. If my happiness is somehow of a different quality than everyone else's, then at least I am internally consistent. But I really don't want to claim this. I just arbitrarily distinguish my happiness from that of others. An arbitrary distinction, however, is an irrational one.

Many people find this simple argument unconvincing, perhaps due to the heavy emphasis our society places on self-interest as a motivator. It may be helpful to think about disutility rather than utility. Almost anyone would grant that it is as bad to do harm to another as to oneself. But why? To be rational, we must justify this view. One possible justification is that if we regard harm as inherently a bad thing, in and of itself, then to be consistent we must try to avoid doing harm to *anyone* (except when it would prevent a greater harm). Harm is harm, regardless of who suffers it. The same argument applies to positive utility.

There are various senses in which I can maximize utility. One is to achieve a *Pareto optimal* state of affairs, which means that if I can do something to make one person happier, without reducing the happiness of anyone else, then I will do it. But maximization is normally understood in the stronger sense that it maximizes the *net sum* of utility across all persons. That is, a small utility loss for one person is outweighed by a greater utility gain for others.

While rationality seems clearly to require a Pareto optimum, it is hard to argue rigorously that it requires maximizing the sum. Nonetheless, I will adopt the working hypothesis that it does. Almost anyone would say that it is better for one person to sacrifice a little if it relieves millions from misery. This follows from the utilitarian test if we take the sum of happiness as the relevant criterion.

- *Utilitarian test. An action is ethical only if no other available action creates greater total net utility.*

It may seem an impossible task to measure happiness in a way that allows us to add it up. But we need only judge whether there is *more* happiness in one outcome than in another. It may not be necessary to arrive at a number that measures the amount of happiness. If alternative A results in a cure for malaria and alternative B a cure for ingrown toenails, we know what to do without putting any numbers on it. When some kind of numerical calculation is necessary, we will see, in the next chapter, that utility theory provides some reasonable ways to do it.

Another issue is that we may want to recognize multiple ends that are desirable for their own sake. Perhaps knowledge, beauty, love, and freedom are valuable irrespective of whether they are associated with happiness or some other good. This raises the problem of how to trade them off when they conflict. Ideally, our goal structure should incorporate some ranking of goals. Value pluralism remains a deep problem and has been the focus of much research in ethics.[2] It is not a major issue, however, in most of the dilemmas analyzed in this book.

A related problem arises when ultimate ends are not universally shared. Perhaps some people find the experience of political freedom or unspoiled wilderness to be intrinsically valuable, apart from whatever pleasure or satisfaction they may bring. It is unclear why these persons should be committed to maximizing freedom or wilderness experiences for those who place no intrinsic value in them. For present purposes, we will suppose that they are obligated to maximize these values only for those who care about them. This matter obviously requires deeper thought for a satisfactory resolution.

## Expected Utility

When the consequences of an action are unpredictable, it may nonetheless be possible to identify a few possible outcomes whose probability can be estimated. One can then calculate the *expected* utility of the action and apply the utilitarian test on that basis.

Suppose, for example, that a farmer is considering whether to plant a crop of wheat. Due to weather and other factors, it is impossible to predict the size of the yield, but the farmer knows from experience that a good year yields a profit of $50,000 and a bad year brings a loss of $20,000. Historically, 30% of years are good years and 70% are bad. If we let profit be a measure of utility, then the expected utility is a weighted sum of the outcomes, where the weights are the probabilities:

$$(0.3)(\$50,000) + (0.7)(-\$20,000) = \$1,000$$

The expected utility can be viewed as the average annual utility that would result over many years. Because the expected utility in this case is positive, planting the crop is (slightly) preferable to planting nothing, from a utilitarian point of view.

## Jennifer's Choice

Jennifer argues that breaking her agreement with Midwest will lead to a better outcome. The job at Midwest doesn't require a person with her unique resume. There are plenty of qualified MBAs who can replace her, and she would be personally unhappy in the Midwest job. Her qualifications and enthusiasm for the Glamour job will create significantly more value for its clients than their second-choice employee would. It is true that she may create a bad reputation for herself at Midwest by breaking her word, and this could prevent her from making the contributions of which she is capable. But Midwest is a small firm in a small city, and we can suppose that its reaction will have minimal effect on her career.

This is a utilitarian argument. Using any reasonable definition of utility, Jennifer can convincingly argue that breaking the agreement will result in at least as much utility as keeping it. She considers her own welfare as well as that of others, but this is appropriate, because everyone's welfare figures into the utilitarian assessment, including hers. Breaking the agreement therefore passes the utilitarian test.

It does not follow, however, that breaking the agreement is ethical. To be ethical, the action must pass *all* the tests for rational choice. Breaking the agreement fails the generalization test and is therefore unethical.

## Does the End Justify the Means?

There is a lingering problem with Jennifer's case, however. Taking the Glamour job not only creates as much utility as taking the Midwest job, but it creates *more* utility. This seems to imply that Jennifer has an obligation to take the Glamour job. Does creating more utility justify breaking the employment agreement with Midwest? Briefly put, does the end justify the means?

Not if the means is unethical on other grounds. The utilitarian test says that an act is ethical only if no other available *act* creates greater utility. Strictly speaking, breaking the agreement with Midwest is not an act because it violates the generalization test and therefore has no consistent rationale. So the utilitarian test does not require Jennifer to take the New York job. Let's restate the utilitarian test to clarify this:

- *Utilitarian test (clarified). An action is ethical only if no other available action creates greater total utility and meets the other conditions for rational choice.*

In other words, the utilitarian test can never *override* another condition for rational choice. All the conditions for rational choice must be met. One should never violate the generalization test to achieve greater utility, no matter how desirable the outcome.

This may seem too strict. One thinks of Jean Valjean, the famous protagonist of Victor Hugo's novel *Les Misérables*, who stole a loaf of bread to feed his starving family. If his theft violates the generalization test, then it is unethical, regardless of what is at stake. But this is a big "if." Remember that the generalization test is applied to the reasons for an action. Stealing a loaf of bread merely to save money is probably ungeneralizable, but Jean Valjean's reasons had a much narrower scope. He stole only because he was penniless and his family was starving. This is a different rationale that may pass the test.

The end never justifies an unethical means, but the means may be ethical if the end is built into the rationale for the act. This was not the case for Jennifer, incidentally. Even if creating greater customer and job satisfaction were part of the rationale for her act, the rationale would still be ungeneralizable.

## Too Much Altruism?

The utilitarian criterion may seem much too demanding. As long as there is poverty and suffering in the world, I can increase utility by giving what I have to the less fortunate. They would gain more than I would lose, until I give so much that I am not much better off than they. Must I impoverish myself to be ethical? This kind of generosity is perhaps laudable, but surely it is not obligatory.

The situation is similar for a business. A wealthy corporation could relieve much suffering through massive charitable contributions to world health, famine relief, and so forth. Certainly, if the company were too generous, it would lose profitability and perhaps go out of business, thereby losing the ability to create any sort of utility. Yet the utilitarian test seems to require it to donate as much as is consistent with its ability to continue making donations and maximize total utility. Few corporations are willing to operate in this mode.

The fact that the utilitarian condition is demanding does not show it is wrong. Yet it only demands that we maximize utility consistent with generalizability. The reason I would impoverish myself to help others is presumably that it would increase total utility. But if everyone who is in a position to increase utility in this fashion did so, there would be too little left to maintain a productive economy. We would have too few resources left to support the infrastructure, educational system, and capital investment necessary to create the kind of wealth I can presently give away. So if sacrificial generosity were generalized, it would not accomplish my purpose of increasing utility and would in fact reduce utility. It therefore fails the test. Note, by the way, that it does not fail the test simply because universal sacrifice would make us worse off. It fails because universal sacrifice is inconsistent with my reason for being sacrificial, which happens to be to increase total utility.

On the other hand, a reasonable degree of generosity is consistent with maintaining a productive economy even when it is generalized. The utilitarian test obligates me to be as generous as I can, subject to the condition that equal generosity on everyone's part would be consistent with achieving the goal of increasing total utility.

The same applies to the owners of a business. They are obligated to contribute as much as possible to causes that increase overall utility, consistent with the ability of the business system to continue to raise capital and support a productive economy if all businesses were equally generous.

## The Role of Self-Interest

Even with all the above qualifications, the utilitarian test may seem to set an unreasonably high standard for mere human beings. While my own utility counts in the utilitarian calculation, every other person's utility receives equal weight. This seems to require me to consider the whole world in every decision. Yet in practice, I find it hard enough to take care of myself, perhaps along with my family and friends.

Ethics never requires us to do what we cannot do (*ought* implies *can*). The utilitarian principle, in particular, asks us to select an *available* action that maximizes utility. An action beyond our powers is not available.

A utilitarian calculation also recognizes that my actions affect me more than anyone else. I have the greatest control over my own affairs, and as a rule, my efforts are more efficiently applied to improving my own situation rather than someone else's. This means I can often maximize utility by placing the greatest emphasis on self-interest.

The balance nonetheless tends to change as I mature and assume greater responsibilities. As a parent, business manager, physician, or teacher, I have substantial influence over the welfare of those in my charge. Utilitarianism requires that they become a more central element of my decision making. Fortunately, maturity tends to bring a greater capacity to meet this responsibility.

A similar principle applies to business. A company creates utility primarily through the efficient and responsible production of valuable goods and services, because this is what it is best equipped to do. More mature companies can and should broaden their perspective, perhaps by contributing to infrastructure and education.

An obligation to care for others may flow from the other conditions of rational choice as well. We have already noted, for example, that professional obligations to stockholders, patients, or students are based on the generalization principle. We will see that the third condition for rational choice can also impose loyalty obligations toward family, coworkers, and others with whom one has a relationship.

## Predicting the Consequences

The utilitarian test asks us to foresee the consequence of an individual action, much as the generalization test asks us to gauge the consequences of a generalized action. Neither requires us to be right about it, but only that we make rational judgments. If I have evidence that action A creates more utility than action B, then consistency requires me to choose action A. However, if the evidence is scarce or ambiguous, and I have no particular reason to believe that one action has better consequences than another, then the utilitarian criterion imposes no particular obligation. Either choice satisfies the utilitarian test.[3]

This doesn't give me a license to be lazy, however. I can't just say that because I happen to have no evidence either way, I can do whatever I want, without trying to gather some evidence. If happiness is my goal, for example, it is irrational for me to act without making some effort to find out how to create happiness. It is as though I want to drive to a certain shop but don't bother to find out which route to take. If I drive around aimlessly, I am simply irrational. It makes no sense to begin the trip without looking at a map or asking a friend about the route.

How much effort must I exert to be rational? It is a trade-off. If I spend too much time studying maps, then I will have too little time to shop when I arrive. To be rational, I must find a balance between information gathering and action that I can reasonably believe maximizes the utility that results.[4]

## Exercises

**19.** In Exercise 7, does boarding early pass the utilitarian test?

**20.** *The accidental bank robbery.*[5] Chris is a relief branch manager for Commerce Trust Bank. His job is to fill in for regular branch managers while they are away. Today he is serving at a bank with several inexperienced tellers. One of them, Carole, comes up $900 short at the end of the day. She is in a panic, because reporting a $900 shortage to headquarters would result in automatic termination of her job. On checking the transactions ledger, Chris finds that while cashing a check, Carole misread $100 as $1,000 and paid out the larger amount. Fortunately, the check holder is one of the bank's best customers. However, when Chris telephones the customer, he insists that he received only $100—even when Chris mentions that Carole would lose her job if the money were not returned. Carole is in tears, but Chris must somehow reconcile the ledger. His options are: (a) report the loss, (b) debit the customer's account by $900, (c) place the amount in a suspense account and let the regular manager resolve the issue at a later time. Which option is likely to maximize utility? *Hint.* If (c) is selected, the regular manager must select (a) or (b).

**21.** *Back at the music shop.* You are again browsing in the music shop that has a CD recording of Arnold Schönberg's *Pierrot Lunaire* on display (see Exercise 11). You were reluctant to steal it last time, but another thought has occurred to you. The shop will never sell this recording, because everyone else in the world hates this atonal stuff, and it can't be returned to the manufacturer. However, if you steal it, at least you will enjoy the music. Furthermore, as a penny-pinching student you can make better use of the $12 on the price tag than the shop owners. The rational thing to do is therefore to steal the CD, if you can get away with it. Is this correct?

**22.** *Irrevocable election.*[6] Steve is in his second year at a CPA firm. A firm partner discovers that Steve neglected to attach an irrevocable election form to one of last year's tax returns. The form is necessary for the client to avoid a substantial tax liability in subsequent years. The partner reassures Steve that it is a fine point he would have not expected Steve to catch. The client shouldn't have to pay a higher tax due to their mistake, but there is a way to fix it. The partner asks Steve to prepare the election form and attach it to their file copy of last year's tax return. Then he is to prepare this year's tax return as though the election form were submitted last year. There is no need to mention any of this to the client. If questions arise, they will show the IRS the file copy of the form and suggest that the IRS lost it in processing. Does the partner's request pass the utilitarian test? Is it ethical?

**23.** *Hard choice in Hondo.*[7] George is manager of an Ardnak Plastics plant in Hondo, Texas. It employs several hundred persons, a large fraction of the local workforce. George's boss, Bill, telephones him from headquarters in El Paso with the news that the EPA will levy fines against Ardnak for excessive smokestack emissions at the Hondo plant. However, Bill won't approve new scrubbers because the company can't afford it. He points out that competitors have escaped EPA fines even though their emissions are higher. Upon investigation, George learns that the competitors avoid fines by scheduling their heavy emissions at night, when the EPA isn't running tests. Meanwhile, Bill has been in touch with the Mexican authorities and mentions to George the possibility of relocating 15 miles south in Mexico, where environmental regulation is lax. This would necessitate hiring Mexican workers and devastate the economy of Hondo. He tells George that he must either avoid the fines or relocate. George therefore has three options: (a) dump the pollution at night, (b) relocate, or (c) resign, in which case his successor will choose (a) because it is the path of least resistance. Assuming that (a) is ungeneralizable, which of these three options pass(es) the utilitarian test?

## VIRTUE ETHICS

The first and second conditions for rational choice impose formal conditions on our decisions. The third condition begins to examine the content of those decisions, while still using rationality as a guide. It says that rational decision making must start by making sense of our role in the world. We can't decide what to do until we decide why we're here.

The resulting guidance is in part purely formal and in part substantive. The purely formal part reminds us that purely formal guidance is not enough. It asks us to subscribe to a cultural tradition, religion, or philosophy that can provide an ultimate basis for decision making. The choice is ours, but however we choose, we must act accordingly. We may also define who we are in part though our choice of career or profession. To be consistent, we must act consistently with this choice.

The second, substantive part begins with the premise that we are rational human beings and deduces that, as such, we must exhibit certain virtues. The resulting guidelines are often called *virtue ethics*. The idea goes back at least to Aristotle and is based on his concept of teleological explanation.

## Teleological Explanation

Teleological explanation is a way of understanding the purpose or function of things. (*Telos*, from the Greek, means purpose.) It is not hard to identify the purpose of artifacts like cars or computers, because their designers give them a purpose. But a teleological approach can help us understand other things as well, such as the human body. It is true that science emphasizes causal explanation. It explains respiration, for example, by identifying a complex chain of chemical reactions. Yet the complexity of the human body would be unintelligible if we did not give it a teleological or functional explanation as well. The function of the heart is to pump blood, the function of the lungs is to provide oxygen to the blood, and so on. The molecular biologists who tell us about chemical reactions acquired their first understanding of the body when their kindergarten teachers told them about the heart and the lungs.

## Virtues

There is an old tradition that finds a purpose for human life in the scheme of things much as we find a purpose for the organs of the body. We say that the heart's function is to pump blood because it is uniquely suited to do so. Similarly, human beings are uniquely suited to certain kinds of activity. We are rational beings. We can apprehend beauty. We are capable of trust, loyalty, friendship, honor, and courage in a self-conscious way that apparently characterizes no other creature. One might conclude that our purpose here is at least in part to bring these qualities to the world. They are traditionally called *virtues*. No one can prove that this is why we are here, but no one can prove that the heart exists to pump blood. Nonetheless it is a hypothesis that helps us make sense of things.

Humans are also uniquely capable of monstrous cruelty, and one may wonder why this would not also be a virtue. Yet no organ of the body can kill like the heart, because a slight electrical disturbance will do the trick. The heart's pumping behavior, not its ability to kill, helps us to understand how the body works. Similarly, cruelty doesn't help us explain human existence but makes that existence even harder to explain. Rather, it is by regarding human beings as the world's source of rationality, aesthetic sensibility, trust, loyalty, honor, friendship, and courage that we are able to make some sense of our predicament.

Another way to put this is that the virtues are part of our *essence*; they help define who we are. A heart can have two chambers or four, but an organ that doesn't pump isn't a heart. A human being can be tall or short or male or female, but a human being without rationality, without any of sense of beauty, with no understanding of friendship, is not fully human.

## Integrity

Integrity (wholeness) is the result of being consistent with who we are. The third condition for rational choice is really an ethic of integrity. We lose integrity when we compromise our honor, abandon a friend, or do a shoddy job that is beneath our intellectual ability. There are various psychological expressions for this: We can't live with ourselves, can't look at ourselves in the mirror, can't sleep at night, and so forth. We are no longer whole persons because we have walked away from who we are as human beings. Yet the third condition does not rely on psychology. It requires us to act in a way that is logically consistently with who we are.

The pressures of business life can make it difficult to develop some of the virtues, such as loyalty and friendship. In Western economies, employees may feel free to depart for greener pastures in the middle of a company project, and the firm may feel free to terminate the employee in mid-career. Workers and managers who share a commitment to each other arguably live fuller lives than those linked only by transitory economic incentives, if only because they can develop their capacity for loyalty and friendship. On the other hand, a competitive business environment encourages one to develop intellectual competence, which is an equally important virtue and equally part of one's essence as a human being.

Virtue ethics tends to be somewhat vague, but in some cases it alone can bring moral clarity. In practice, its applicability depends on whether virtues conflict. If a single virtue is at stake, then it must not be compromised, unless this would require an ungeneralizable act. If conflicting virtues are at issue, however, virtue ethics may provide no clear directive.

Virtue ethics sometimes seems to conflict with the generalization principle. Family loyalty, as well as utility maximization, may require Jean Valjean to commit a seemingly ungeneralizable act of theft. This is an old conundrum and a perennial subject of literature.[8] It is harder to resolve than apparent conflicts with the utilitarian principle, which calls only for utility maximization within limits set by the other principles.

We will deal with this matter by supposing that virtue ethics cannot override the generalization principle. One justification for this is that virtue ethics is rather vague in the first place, and the generalization principle helps resolve the vagueness. Another is that an act may be generalizable when preserving virtue is one of the reasons for it, thus removing the conflict. A deeper understanding of ethics is necessary to resolve this issue completely, but it is only occasionally a pivotal factor in business decisions.

### Jennifer's Choice

A virtue ethics perspective would argue for Jennifer's accepting a job in which she could develop her abilities, such as the Glamour Finance job. Walking away from Midwest Consulting is perhaps not a breach of loyalty, either, because no relationship has really been established. On the other hand, a breach of agreement would compromise Jennifer's honor and integrity. Honor is part of integrity, because it is part of who we are.

It is never consistent to act contrary to a virtue, unless it is for the sake of another virtue. In this case, however, there is a conflict of virtues, and virtue ethics provides no clear verdict. The best Jennifer can do is to try to strike a balance. The ancient Greeks viewed the ability to find a balance as itself a virtue, which they called *sophrosyne* (a word with no English equivalent).

In this case, the best compromise may be to stay with Midwest, where Jennifer can still look for opportunities to develop her talents to the utmost. For example, with sufficient cleverness and persistence she may persuade the company to introduce a new analysis tool that will better serve customers and perhaps attract national attention. On the other hand, if she leaves Midwest, there is little she can do to mitigate her loss of honor.

The following scorecard sums up the ethics of breaking the Midwest employment contract:

1. Generalization test: *Fail.*
2. Utilitarian test: *Pass.*
3. Virtue ethics test: Inconclusive, but leaning toward *fail.*

Because an act must meet all the conditions to be ethical, breaking the contract is unethical.

## Exercises

**24.** *Retirement fund recommendation.*[9] John is a portfolio analyst for Metropolitan City Teachers' Retirement Fund (MCTRF). His boss Mary has asked him to compare one of MCTRF's external growth stock portfolio managers, Bill Fredericks, against Growth Unlimited (GU) and make a recommendation. Mary sees some impressive numbers in GU's performance over the last three years. In fact, John normally evaluates fund managers based on a three-year record. However, this time he is considering a different approach. Bill Fredericks was actually slightly ahead of GU last quarter. In addition, John and Bill have become close friends. Bill has helped John with several projects apart from growth stock investing and has arranged for John and his staff to attend some of Bill's educational seminars without cost to MCTRF. Analyze John's decision from a virtue ethics perspective. Which recommendation(s) pass the virtue ethics test?

**25.** *Plant automation.*[10] George is a recent MBA who just joined a manufacturing firm's Cedar Valley plant as its only cost accountant. Cedar Valley is a town of 20,000 people, and the plant is one of several owned by the firm. George's boss Arthur tells him that management wants to automate this particular plant with robots as a pilot project, to help judge whether the other plants should be automated. Arthur admits that the community will be in an uproar due to the loss of jobs. However, the firm can save some of the jobs through retraining. Once George releases accounting information showing that the upgrade is necessary, the community will be less likely to resist. George points out that the report he sent to headquarters last year found that automation would not benefit the plant. Yet Arthur points out that the report was based on cost assumptions, and these can be adjusted as necessary to make the bottom line come out differently. After all, market prices fluctuate, and there is no solid proof that one cost estimate is better than another. How does virtue ethics bear on this case?

**26.** *Missing travel documentation.*[11] Tim, a CPA, works for an auditing firm and has been placed in charge of an annual audit for Dalton Enterprises, a medium-sized firm with $20 million in assets. Mr. Dalton micromanages the family-owned firm except the finance area, which he leaves to his son Chauncy, recently appointed as VP of Finance. Chauncy's duties include the appointment of auditors. Past audit reports have never been circulated outside the firm. They have been quite detailed, including all changes in general ledger accounts, because Mr. Dalton uses the reports for administrative control purposes. Tim notices that travel expenses are $20,000 higher this year, due to expenditures authorized by Chauncy. Most of these expenses are undocumented, but the firm's controller seems unconcerned. Tim finally raises the issue with Chauncy, who questions why auditors would be skeptical of his honesty. He says that it is typical of "bean counters" to focus on minor issues while ignoring possibilities for major efficiency improvements. He ends the interview by asking, "What are we paying you guys for anyhow?" How does virtue ethics relate to Tim's decision as to what to put in the report?

**27.** *The good credit reference.*[12] Diversified Consolidated Corporation (DCC) is a supplier for North Manufacturing. As a credit officer at DCC, Kathy is responsible for about $1 million in credits to North. There are rumors that North is in deep trouble. The company has always paid on time and even lists BCC as a credit reference. Nonetheless, Kathy decides that a visit with North's treasurer, Scott, is in order. They have developed a good working relationship over the years, and after a few drinks at lunch, Scott levels with her. He confesses that although North's latest financial statements are technically correct, there has been a sudden reversal, and the company is talking to bankruptcy attorneys. Scott is giving first priority to paying suppliers like DCC, because supplier credit is their only hope for survival. In fact, Scott has just placed a major order with DCC's competitor Basic Products. If there is anything Kathy can do to convince Basic to extend credit, North may get over this hump and bring business back to DCC. Otherwise, North is probably headed for bankruptcy by the end of the quarter. Later that day, Kathy receives a phone call from her friend Mike at Basic Products. Suppliers often share credit information, and Mike asks about North. He has heard rumors, and he wants to make sure all is well before he commits to a major order. He is relieved when Kathy tells him that North continues to make its payments promptly. She asks him to hold the line a moment. Her mind races as she thinks about whether to tell the rest of the story. How does virtue ethics interact with the other conditions for rational choice in this case?

28. Suppose that in Exercise 22, the partner thinks better of committing tax fraud. Instead, he tells Steve that the firm will cover the portion of the client's tax bill that results from Steve's mistake. However, it's best that the client know nothing of this. Steve is therefore asked to send the client a copy of the tax form he would have prepared to carry out the partner's first plan, rather than the form actually submitted to the IRS. The partner points out that his new plan complies with tax law and benefits the client, so it can't be unethical. Is he right?

29. What is the ethical choice in Exercise 20?

## Notes

1. Based on the Arthur Andersen mini-case *Damage Expense* by Michael Forget and Raymond L. Hilgert. A number of the exercises in this book are based on a collection of ethics case studies assembled by Arthur Andersen & Co. S.C. during the period 1987–1994. They were one product of a $5 million effort by Andersen to raise awareness of ethical issues in business. Ironically, Andersen surrendered its CPA licenses and effectively went out of business in 2002 when convicted of obstruction of justice for its role in the Enron scandal (the U.S. Supreme Court overturned the conviction in 2005). The case collection consists of five full-length case studies and 85 mini-cases.

2. For example, Isaac Levi, *Hard Choices: Decision Making under Unresolved Conflict*, Cambridge University Press, 1990.

3. This differs from classical utilitarianism, which requires me to choose the action that actually maximizes utility. The classical theory is consequentialist, while the theory presented here is a deontological reinterpretation of utilitarianism.

4. This is related to the concept of *bounded rationality* introduced by my former colleague Herbert Simon. For Simon, bounded rationality is a corrective for rational agent models in economics. It takes into account the fact that human beings have limited knowledge and ability to choose rational acts, even acts that are rational in the narrow, self-interested sense used by economists. Yet Simon acknowledged

that we can be completely rational when acting without full knowledge, because we may have reason to believe that further investment in fact-finding could consume more effort than it is potentially worth (or to use a term from decision theory, the *net expected value of perfect information* is negative).

5. Based on the Arthur Andersen mini-case *The Accidental Bank Robbery* by D. Anthony Plath.

6. Based on the Arthur Andersen mini-case *Irrevocable Election* by Ed Scribner.

7. Based on the Arthur Andersen mini-case *Something Rotten in Hondo* by John Fraedrich.

8. One thinks of Søren Kierkegaard's analysis of Abraham's decision in the biblical book of Genesis to sacrifice his son at God's command. Kierkegaard calls it a "teleological suspension of the ethical" in his book *Fear and Trembling* (1843). In our terms, it would be a teleological suspension of the generalization principle.

9. Based on the Arthur Andersen mini-case *Metropolitan City Teachers' Retirement Fund Performance Appraisal* by James R. Haltiner and Paul B. Bursik.

10. Based on the Arthur Andersen mini-case *Plant Automation* by Sue Atkinson.

11. Based on the Arthur Andersen mini-case *What Happened to All Those Credit Slips?* by Robert R. Davis.

12. Based on the Arthur Andersen mini-case *The Good Credit Reference* by Scott B. Moore and Edward D. Curren.

# Chapter *3*

# Distributive Justice and Autonomy

Many if not most organizational decisions allocate resources. People want their fair share, and decision makers are frequently called upon to justify their allocations. If the principles of rational choice are to be adequate for real-world decision making, they must provide guidance for just distribution.

The utilitarian principle has obvious relevance. It asks us to distribute resources so that they do the most good. This raises the issue of how to calculate the resulting utility, and it may seem a hopeless task to quantify such ultimate ends as happiness. Yet it can be done well enough for practical purposes, and it is not as hard as one might think. This chapter shows how.

Maximizing utility is not the whole story, however. The utilitarian principle tends to allocate the lion's share of resources to the most productive individuals, because they create more utility. Those who are left out may insist that they deserve a decent standard of living, even if they are less productive due to life circumstances over which they have little control, such as illness, disability, unemployment, and a disadvantaged background, or assignment to a job that is inherently less productive.

We approach this issue through the well-known ethical principles of John Rawls, which are based on essentially the same reasoning as the generalization principle. We do not attempt to follow Rawlsian thought precisely but use it as a starting point for developing the tools we need for rational choice.

This foray into Rawlsian philosophy will provide an opportunity to elaborate on a central idea that has only been briefly discussed—the autonomy of a moral agent. Autonomy not only explains why actions must be based on reasons, but respecting autonomy is itself a moral imperative. It lies behind much of what we say about the value of life and freedom and the immorality of coercion and oppression.

## MEASURING UTILITY

The utilitarian test assumes that there is some way to measure the utility of one outcome versus the utility of another. But how can we assign a number to someone's happiness or satisfaction? Even if we can do this, does it make sense to add up these numbers across different people?

As noted in the previous chapter, common sense suffices to settle many cases. We used common sense to measure utility in Jennifer's dilemma, for example. In business decisions, wealth can often serve as a reasonable surrogate for utility, particularly if great disparities of wealth are not part of the picture. We know how to measure wealth. Even when this is inadequate, elementary utility theory provides a workable approach.

The idea can be illustrated by a real case. In 1996, AT&T laid off about 40,000 workers, including some 17,000 managers, typically middle-aged. Every option available to AT&T at the time was harmful to someone. Layoffs would harm the redundant workers, but a bloated payroll would harm the company and therefore everyone that depended on it. The utilitarian test asks whether the layoff would result in gains that outweigh the losses.

Measuring total net wealth is probably not adequate in this case. Even if stockholders gain more wealth than laid-off workers lose, one might argue that the workers lose more utility than the stockholders gain. The workers' salary may be worth more to them than a gain in share price is worth to stockholders. We will analyze the situation with the concept of an individual *utility function* that measures the value of wealth.

## Utility Functions

Classical utility theory assumes that everyone has a utility function $u(Q)$ that measures the utility of possessing wealth $Q$. A typical utility function appears in Figure 3.1, where the horizontal axis represents wealth (perhaps annual salary) and the vertical axis the utility of that wealth. The curve is concave (i.e., less steep at the high end) because wealth has greater marginal value when one has less of it. Figure 3.2 illustrates that a gain of $10,000 benefits someone with $20,000 income more than its loss harms someone with $100,000 income.

Suppose the AT&T layoff results in income $Q_i$ for each person $i$. Then the total utility that results from the layoff is $\Sigma_i u(Q_i)$, the sum of the resulting utilities over all persons affected. Next suppose that retaining these employees results in income $Q_i'$ for each person $i$, which will be higher than $Q_i$ for those who would have been laid off, but lower for some others. The utilitarian test says that the layoff is preferable if it results in greater total utility, that is, if $\Sigma_i u(Q_i) > \Sigma_i u(Q_i')$.

## Calibrating Utility Functions

The utilitarian calculation obviously requires that we know what utility curves look like. There is a simple way to find out. Let's suppose you want to calibrate your utility function $u$. Pretend that you make $100,000 at AT&T and are asked to choose between two alternatives: (a) keeping your job with a lower salary of $Q$ and (b) retaining your current salary, but with a 50–50 chance you

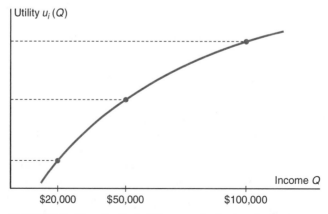

**FIGURE 3.1** Hypothetical utility curve for income levels.

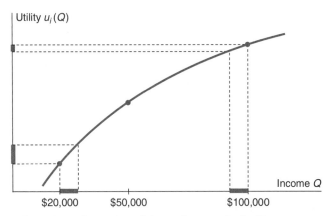

**FIGURE 3.2**   Illustration of decreasing marginal utility.

will lose your job and have to work elsewhere for $20,000. Now ask yourself, for what value of Q are you indifferent between these two alternatives?

Let's suppose you are indifferent when Q = $50,000. Then the expected utility of (a) and (b) should be the same for you. If you choose job security, your utility is $u(50,000)$, the value of your utility function at $50,000. If you choose the lottery with a 50–50 chance of losing your job, your expected utility is a weighted average of the utilities of the two outcomes, where the weights are their probabilities (½ for each). This yields the equation

$$u(50,000) \; = \; \frac{1}{2}\,u(100,000) \; + \; \frac{1}{2}\,u(20,000) \tag{1}$$

You can arbitrarily assign numbers to the utility of $100,000 and of $20,000. They can be any numbers you want, but let's say $u(100,000) = 40$ and $u(20,000) = 10$. Equation (1) now determines the utility of $50,000 to be 25.

You can carry out the same thought experiment for other probabilities. Let $p$ be the probability you will lose your job if you retain your current salary, which means $1 - p$ is the probability you will keep it. You decide that you are indifferent between this lottery and a secure job with salary Q. Then the expected utilities are again the same for the two options:

$$u(Q) \; = \; (1 - p)u(100,000) \; + \; pu(20,000) \tag{2}$$

By evaluating the right-hand side of equation (2), you can derive the utility of Q. Two of the utility values are arbitrary, but once you fix them, all the others are determined.

You can continue these thought experiments for several probabilities $p$ and identify several points on the graph of your utility function. (Or you could try several values of Q and identify the corresponding probabilities $p$.) By connecting the points with a smooth curve, you have an approximation of your utility function.[1]

The specific numerical values of the utility function have no meaning, because you could have started with any distinct values for $u(20,000)$ and $u(100,000)$. But *relative utility differences* mean something. Losing your job reduces utility twice as much as getting a 50% pay cut, no matter what values you assign to $u(20,000)$ and $u(100,000)$. This is verified in Mathematical Note 1 at the end of the chapter.

For practical purposes, it is normally adequate to suppose that everyone has more or less the same utility function. Also, because relative utility differences are meaningful, it makes sense to compare the total utility of two alternatives. Even if the utility function were calibrated with different starting values, the utilitarian decision would always be the same.

Thus, we have all the tools we need for AT&T to apply the utilitarian test. Carrying out the analysis is quite practical. A company economist can suggest a reasonable utility function. Other company analysts can estimate the financial impact of the two options on stakeholders, or may have already done so. The rest can be done on a spreadsheet. If some stakeholders dispute the decision that results, which is very likely, the company is now in a position to explain why its choice is best all around.

The situation is more difficult when different stakeholder groups have significantly different utility functions. The interpersonal comparability of utility functions has received a good deal of study that goes beyond the scope of this book. Nonetheless, the principal lesson to take away from this section is that utilitarian calculations are often possible and practical in business contexts.

## Exercises

1. You wish to estimate the utility to you of earning the annual salaries in the left column of Table 3.1. You fix the utility of $10,000 arbitrarily at 15, and the utility of $40,000 arbitrarily at 25. You decide that you are indifferent between (a) receiving a sure salary of $Q$ between $10,000 and $40,000 and (b) taking a chance of receiving $40,000 with probability $p$ and $10,000 with probability $1 - p$, where $Q$ and $p$ are shown in the table. Calculate the utility of salaries $15,000, $20,000, and $30,000.

2. Now suppose you wish to estimate the utility of $5,000. You are indifferent between (a) receiving $10,000 for sure and (b) receiving $40,000 with probability $p$ and $5,000 with probability $1 - p$, where $p = 1/3$. Use this to calculate the utility of $5,000.

   *Hint.* Suppose, in general, that you fix utilities for salaries $Q_1$ and $Q_2$ (here, $10,000 and $40,000, respectively) and wish to calculate the utility of some salary $Q$ that is less than $10,000. If you are indifferent between (a) receiving $Q_1$ and (b) a lottery in which you receive $Q_2$ with probability $p$ and $Q$ with probability $1 - p$, then

$$u(Q_1) = (1 - p)u(Q) + pu(Q_2)$$

   This allows you to solve for $u(Q)$ in terms of $u(Q_1)$ and $u(Q_2)$.

3. Suppose you are indifferent between (a) receiving a salary of $40,000 for sure and (b) a lottery in which you receive $50,000 with probability $p$ and $10,000 with probability $1 - p$, where $p = 0.9$. Use this fact to calculate the utility of $50,000.

4. Plot your utility curve using the results of the previous three exercises.

| TABLE 3.1 | Data for Exercises 1–4 | |
| --- | --- |
| **Salary $Q$** | **Probability $p$** |
| 15,000 | 0.35 |
| 20,000 | 0.6 |
| 30,000 | 0.85 |

## DISTRIBUTIVE JUSTICE

An allocation may be unjust even when it maximizes utility. True, there is already a principle of justice in utilitarianism simply because everyone's utility is given equal weight in the calculation. One cannot (arbitrarily) give greater weight to members of the upper class or of a certain race, for example. Furthermore, utilitarian solutions show at least some preference for equality because utility curves are concave, and resources are worth more at the margin to those who have less (Figure 3.2). This can partially offset the advantage of allocating most of the resources to a few more productive persons (see Mathematical Note 2).

But utilitarian calculations nonetheless endorse highly unequal and possibly unjust distributions if they happen to maximize overall utility. They may require us to pay CEOs exorbitant salaries while paying sweatshop laborers next to nothing, deny health care benefits to low-wage workers, refuse to hire the handicapped, and so forth, if these policies raise the average utility despite hurting those at the low end. To determine whether these policies are ethical, we must apply the other conditions for rational choice.

### The Veil of Ignorance

John Rawls proposed a vivid way of understanding the generalizability of reasons.[2] On his view, you must make a decision *without knowing who you are.* When Jennifer decides to sign with Glamour, for example, she could be Jennifer, a manager at Midwest, or another student. As Rawls put it, she must decide behind a "veil of ignorance" as to her station in life. She will find out who she is only after she makes the decision. Her reasons must justify her choice no matter who she turns out to be.

This can be seen as one more consequence of the generalization principle. The principle can be understood as requiring that a decision be evaluated as a policy for everyone. But this means (a) the reasons must be consistent with everyone's carrying out the policy (the generalization test), and (b) the policy must be rational from everyone's point of view (the Rawlsian test).

The Rawlsian test does not mean that one should figure the probabilities and maximize the expected outcome when one learns one's identity. An AT&T executive behind the veil of ignorance might decide it is a good bet to lay off some middle-aged employees to make a company more profitable. She might be one of those terminated, but there is a greater chance she would be someone who benefits from the layoff. She is willing to take her chances. Rawls says this is not enough. She must construct a justification for the layoff that would be equally rational for her to use if she were transported into the body of one of the redundant employees.

### The Difference Principle

Rawls used his idea of the veil of ignorance to analyze distributive justice. He arrived at two principles:

- *Liberty Principle*: A policy must result in the greatest basic liberty for everyone.
- *Difference Principle*: A policy must not create inequality unless it results in the greatest benefit for the least advantaged.

The Liberty Principle addresses the issue of autonomy, which we take up in the next section. The Difference Principle applies to allocations of utility, such as salary levels. Because the principle is a generalization test, it evaluates a company's salary scale as though it were general policy for all companies: Certain types of work earn certain types of compensation. The Difference Principle says that it is unjust to create salary differentials unless the lowest paid would be even worse off if all salaries were equal. Perhaps there would be no incentive for people to work hard or prepare themselves for the more responsible positions. Companies would become much less profitable, and possibly go under, making the lowest salaries even lower (perhaps zero). If this is true, then salary differences of some sort are necessary to make the lowest-paid person as well off as possible and therefore satisfy the Difference Principle.

The Difference Principle has been defended with a social contract argument. We all get together and make policy before we know who we are. A policy is justified only if we can all rationally agree with it after finding out how we will be personally affected. But I can rationally agree with a policy that puts me on the bottom only if I would have been even worse off under another policy. In other words, it is rational to minimize regret. The policy must therefore result in the greatest possible benefit to those on the bottom.

## Refining the Difference Principle

The Difference Principle requires several clarifications before it can be applied. First, the principle doesn't say that a policy should maximize benefit to those *currently* on the bottom. The argument from rational choice clearly implies that it should result in the greatest possible benefit to those on the bottom after the allocation. This is sometimes referred to as a *maximin* principle, because it maximizes the resulting minimum.

It is also unclear what it means to "create inequality." If an action raises the welfare of the middle class, for example, it widens the gap between the middle and the bottom but reduces the gap between the middle and the top. Does this create or reduce inequality? Perhaps the best way to deal with this issue is simply to say that we should maximize the welfare of the worst off, whether or not we "create" inequality. A party to a social contract would want to minimize regret whether the inequality results from the contract or from some other source.

- Revised Difference Principle: *A policy must result in the greatest benefit for those who are least advantaged after the policy is generally adopted.*

Still another question is whether the "least advantaged" should refer to an individual person or a group. Should we maximize the welfare of the poorest individual, or the lowest class in general? It seems best to say that the Difference Principle refers to the smallest group whose welfare is actually controlled by the allocation.

For example, if I sell lottery tickets, I don't maximize the welfare of the worst-off ticket holder, because the losers would have been better off if I had sold no tickets. Yet my choice to sell lottery tickets didn't make any particular person worse off. That person could just as well have been the winner, under the same choice. On the other hand, the decision to have a lottery controls the welfare of ticket holders as a group. In fact, it makes them worse off, because I keep part of the proceeds of the lottery tickets. A policy of holding lotteries of a given type therefore passes the Difference Principle unless the tickets holders are, as a group, the least-advantaged persons.

For similar reasons, a company is not required to maximize the wealth of its poorest employee, because the company controls only the salaries. Even if all salaries were equal, different levels of wealth would result due to different spending habits and personal circumstances. However, the average welfare of all employees receiving low salaries may be predictable. Companies are required only to choose a salary scale that, if generally adopted, would maximize the collective welfare of those receiving the lowest salaries.

The Difference Principle is sometimes strengthened to say that after maximizing the welfare of the worst-off group, we should then maximize the welfare of the second worst-off group (without reducing the welfare of the worst off). The social contract argument would seem to require that those who end up second from the bottom minimize regret, as well as those on the bottom. We should then maximize the welfare of the third worst-off group, and so forth. This is known as *lexicographic maximization* because of an analogy with putting words in lexicographic (i.e., alphabetical) order. One alphabetizes by the first letter (analogous with the worst-off group), then by the second letter, and so forth.

- **Extended Difference Principle:** *A policy must result in a lexicographic maximum of benefits after the policy is generally adopted.*

What kind of benefits are subject to the Difference Principle? Rawls says that it applies only to "primary goods," which he defines as things that everyone wants, no matter what else they want. These include income, wealth, and rights and prerogatives other than the basic liberties guaranteed by the Liberty Principle. It is important that everyone want the benefits, because otherwise the social contract argument would not go through. I don't care whether I end up on the bottom if I have no interest in the benefits allocated.

To be consistent with our framework, we will view the Difference Principle as applying to allocations of *utility*, as defined in Chapter 2. This means that the principle applies to what we regard as intrinsically valuable, perhaps happiness or pleasure. The social contract argument remains valid to the extent that these are universally valued. In practice, we typically focus on benefits that enhance these intrinsic goods, such as income and health, just as when applying the utilitarian principle. This tends to yield similar results as focusing on primary goods (except that Rawls doesn't regard health as a primary good). If the kind of utility at stake is not universally seen as an intrinsic value, such as wilderness experience, then we consider only those who value it intrinsically, as we do when using the utilitarian principle.

Some people are uncomfortable with the Difference Principle. It implies, for example, that salary scales should maximize the welfare of those in the lowest bracket, even if paying more to top executives would result in greater total income. Some say that the utilitarian principle should prevail on such cases and that top executives should earn a thousand times more than the average worker if this maximizes aggregate utility (accounting for the concavity of utility curves).

The social contract argument for the Difference Principle is perhaps less than airtight. Yet the argument (if any) for maximizing total utility, as opposed to obtaining a Pareto optimum, is even less certain. Both principles are working approximations. Perhaps at some point we will discover a synthesis of the two that can be rigorously defended.

In the meantime, rationality constrains those who reject the Difference Principle to be clear about why the social contract argument doesn't work. They must also be prepared to accept the consequences of having no distributive justice principle, or else find a defensible substitute. For example, they must endorse social arrangements in which an underclass toils for privileged elites, or the physically and mentally impaired are left out of the economy, if such arrangements maximize total utility consistent with generalizability and virtue ethics.

## The Liberty Principle

The Liberty Principle might be defended on the grounds that agency itself requires a certain amount of freedom to achieve one's purposes. There can be no consistent rationale for destroying agency, because having a rationale for any action presupposes the ability to choose one's actions. This justifies giving the Liberty Principle priority over the Difference Principle. When designing an allocation, the first task is to make sure that everyone has basic liberty, if possible, at which point remaining benefits can be distributed in a way consistent with the Difference Principle.

The Liberty Principle protects *basic* liberty, not the freedom to do anything we want. Its most obvious consequence is that it is wrong to cause death, unless other lives are at stake. The same applies to debilitating injury, imprisonment, coercion, or otherwise consigning people to a situation in which they have no meaningful control over their lives, unless these are necessary to avoid equal or greater deprivation for others. Further examples might include slave labor or extreme sweatshop conditions that rob people of any meaningful alternatives.

It is also wrong to deprive people of the faculties necessary to make rational choices, perhaps by means of a psychoactive drug, psychological manipulation, overbearing indoctrination, or denial of opportunity for cognitive development—because without rationality, there is no agency. Thus, an advertising campaign that works subconsciously could be examined for possible violations of the Liberty Principle.

The obvious question arises as to what to do when we must take the life or liberty of some for the sake of others. This quandary arises when a drug saves many lives but will inevitably destroy a few due to unintended side effects, or when we incarcerate criminals to prevent harm to future victims. The unfortunate fact is that the Liberty Principle, as I interpret it, doesn't tell us how to balance one life against another. If the available options are generalizable and consistent with virtue ethics, we must treat life and liberty as forms of utility and select the option that maximizes utility. This may force us to put some kind of value on life, however unpleasant that may be.

In fact, it is common to assign a monetary value to human life in contexts where there is no other way to make a rational decision. A government might avoid all deaths by severe weather, for example, by investing billions in every conceivable safeguard, but only at the cost of shutting down other services, perhaps including those that save life and limb. This seems clearly irrational, and the only evident alternative is to assign a monetary cost to death and injury.

## Exercises

5. A drug is discovered that cures all mild cases of diabetes but has no effect on severe cases. It is therefore prescribed only for patients who have mild cases. Does this policy satisfy the Difference Principle?
6. Suppose the drug in the previous exercise cures all mild cases but has only a small positive effect on severe cases. The drug is in short supply, and to make the best use of it, it is prescribed only for patients with mild cases. Does this policy satisfy the Difference Principle?
7. Some provincial governments conduct daily lotteries. Studies have found that those who buy the lottery tickets are the poorest people in the province. Does this type of lottery satisfy the Difference Principle?
8. *An economics game.*[3] A popular economics game teaches an important lesson in rationality. You are granted $100 along with the option of donating any portion of the grant (from $0 to $100) to an anonymous person. That person, to whom the donor is anonymous, is given the option of accepting or rejecting the donation. If the gift is rejected, both parties forfeit the money. No collusion is allowed. Clearly, rational self-interest requires that you donate a very small positive amount (say, one cent) and that the recipient accept it. If you donated zero, the recipient could reject it without penalty, but it is irrational to turn down even one cent. Actual behavior is quite different. The average donation tends to be in the range of $30–40, and close to half give away $50. This behavior is normally cited as a demonstration that people are irrational. Yet this follows only if rationality is interpreted in the narrow sense of rational self-interest. How can the observed behavior, particular the behavior of those who donate half the money, be seen as entirely rational from a Rawlsian perspective?

## MATHEMATICAL NOTE 1

When a utility function $u_i$ is calibrated by the lottery method described in this chapter, the ratio of utility losses is the same, no matter what initial values are used to calibrate the function. Let's suppose that initial values are assigned to $u_i(Q_1)$ and $u_i(Q_3)$, where $Q_1 = 20,000$ and $Q_3 = 100,000$

in the example of Figure 3.2. The utility loss of a salary cut from $Q_3$ to some intermediate value $Q_2$ ($50,000 in the example) is $u_i(Q_3) - u_i(Q_2)$, and the utility loss of a cut from $Q_3$ to $Q_1$ is $u_i(Q_3) - u_i(Q_1)$. The ratio of these losses is

$$\frac{u_i(Q_3) - u_i(Q_2)}{u_i(Q_3) - u_i(Q_1)}$$

Because individual $i$ is indifferent between a secure salary of $Q_2$ and a lottery between $Q_1$ and $Q_3$ for some probability $p$, we can write $u_i(Q_2) = (1 - p)u_i(Q_1) + pu_i(Q_3)$. We substitute this expression for $u_i(Q_2)$ in the above ratio and get

$$\frac{(1 - p)u_i(Q_3) - (1 - p)u_i(Q_1)}{u_i(Q_3) - u_i(Q_1)}$$

But this algebraically simplifies to $1 - p$. So the ratio is the same (namely, $1 - p$) regardless of what arbitrary values are initially assigned to $u_i(Q_1)$ and $u_i(Q_3)$.

## MATHEMATICAL NOTE 2

The utilitarian bias toward equality is limited, as shown by a mathematical analysis. Suppose for the sake of argument that the utility generated by a person $i$ who receives resources $Q$ is given by $c_i Q^p$. This reflects not just the utility of $Q$ to individual $i$, but the utility of what individual $i$ will accomplish with resources $Q$. The exponent $p$ is less than 1 when there are decreasing marginal returns. The coefficient $c_i$ indicates the individual's ability to use the resources; $c_i$ is presumably larger for individuals who are intelligent, well positioned in society, or advantaged in other ways. The goal is to maximize $\sum_i c_i Q_i^p$ subject to $\sum_i Q_i = R$, where $Q_i$ is the amount of resource allocated individual $i$ and $R$ is the total amount of resource available. If $p = 1$ (i.e., marginal utility is constant), then the most advantaged person gets all of the resources. Otherwise the problem can be solved by associating Lagrange multiplier $\lambda$ with the constraint. The optimal solution satisfies the Lagrangean equations $pc_i Q_i^{p-1} = \lambda$ for each $i$ and $\sum_i Q_i = R$. It is therefore

$$Q_i = R\, \frac{c_i^{1/(1-p)}}{\sum_j c_j^{1/(1-p)}}$$

This gives more resources to the more gifted persons but no longer gives everything to the most gifted. As the exponent $p$ drops to 0, the allocation becomes proportional to $c_i$. So the most nearly equal distribution that a utilitarian can endorse is to give each person resources in proportion to that person's ability to use them.

## Notes

1. Or you could use regression techniques to fit a reasonable functional form to the points, perhaps $u_i(Q) = \alpha + \beta Q^r$. The regression procedure determines the values of $\alpha$, $\beta$, and $r$ that result in the best fit.

2. John Rawls, *A Theory of Justice*, Harvard University Press, 1971, last revision 1999.

3. This version of the game is used by Edward Fischer, an anthropologist at Vanderbilt University, although the interpretation is mine.

# Chapter 4

# Initial Case Studies

This chapter provides some initial examples of how ethical dilemmas may be analyzed using the principles of rational choice. The object here is not to conduct a thorough or lengthy analysis of every case but to illustrate at an elementary level how the principles apply.

## Spying on Unilever

### SYNOPSIS[1]

In 2001, John Pepper, the then Chairman of the Board at Procter and Gamble (P&G), discovered that contractors for his company had been spying on a competitor, Unilever. They had been digging through trash bins outside Unilever's Chicago offices in hope of finding memos that revealed the company's marketing strategy. They took some 80 documents related to hair care products. Pepper was outraged by the practice and fired the contractors. He confessed the action to Unilever, returned the documents, and pledged not to use the information in them. Although P&G's spying was not criminal behavior, Unilever responded by playing hardball. It demanded $20 million in damages, reassignment of some P&G hair care managers, and restrictions on the marketing of some of its hair care products. It further demanded that P&G submit to a third-party auditor who would ensure that the company did not act on the information in the documents. Reporters asked a spokesman for The Society of Competitive Intelligence Professionals about the ethics of P&G's behavior. He responded that the society's Code of Ethics condones trash scavenging only when the trash bins are on public property.

### THE ISSUE

Did John Pepper overreact? Industrial espionage is practiced worldwide, and industrial spies even have a professional organization with its own code of ethics. Perhaps there was nothing wrong with

spying on Unilever, in which case there was no need for Pepper to confess and get his company into serious trouble.

As for the "professional" code of ethics, it is unhelpful. The proviso that bins be located on public property is presumably based on the illegality of taking anything of value from private property. This does not address the issue of whether spying is ethical. If it is wrong, then it is wrong whether carried out on public property or private property.

### ANALYSIS

It is often useful to begin by analyzing a clearer case, to learn lessons that may help to understand a more difficult case. We can therefore begin by exploring the ethics of a more egregious case of spying, as when an employee sells information about his company to a competitor. The generalization test has a clear verdict. The reason for the spy's actions presumably is to make some money. If all employees who could make money by selling confidential information did so, then they would no longer have access to the information. Companies would make sure that sensitive information is carefully controlled and entrusted to as few trusted employees as possible. The spy would no longer be able to make any money by selling information. Spying of this kind is therefore ungeneralizable.

Moving to the issue of spying in trash bins, it is ungeneralizable for a similar reason. If companies routinely searched through trash bins for information, that information would be routinely shredded. It would no longer be possible to achieve the purposes of the action. (In fact, shredding has become common practice.)

A utilitarian analysis is harder to carry out, because it is hard to predict the overall net effect of spying. Yet there is no need to carry it out, because P&G's actions violate generalizability and are unethical on that ground alone.

We can say something about how virtue ethics applies to this case, even though this is unnecessary to resolve it. The trash scavenging was carried out by a marketing firm, presumably staffed by marketing professionals. The mission of the marketing profession is not simply to sell a product, but to match supply and demand.

Marketing professionals find out what goods and services people need or want, so that firms produce them rather than something else. Digging through trash for confidential information doesn't further this mission and is therefore contrary to what being a marketing professional should be all about.

The scorecard for P&G's spying is as follows:

1. Generalization test: *Fail.*
2. Utilitarian test: Not applied.
3. Virtue ethics test: *Fail.*

John Pepper's outrage was justified. ▨

## Exercises

1. Suppose that when John Pepper discovered the espionage, he also discovered that very similar information appeared in the business media the day before the trash bins were raided. How does the analysis change?
2. In the previous exercise, suppose that shortly after the Unilever story appeared, other media outlets reported that the journalist paid a Unilever insider for the information, and the insider was fired.
3. Suppose that P&G acquires secret Unilever marketing plans from an attached file that a Unilever employee mistakenly sends to a P&G employee.
4. In the previous exercise, suppose that the attached file is deliberately sent to P&G from a disgruntled Unilever employee who was fired for some other reason.
5. Is all spying wrong? For example, is spying on another country for national security generalizable?
6. *Spy or customer?*[2] Business Equipment Corporation (BEC) has developed a new technology that will enable it to launch a fax machine superior to anything now on the market. Kyle, product manager at BEC, goes into panic when he reads that Hiyota, a competitor, plans to release a new high-quality fax machine before BEC's product will be ready. Kyle must find out what the machine can do as soon as possible, so he can give the production department new specifications if necessary. He asks his marketing consultant Lynn to make an appointment with a Hiyota sales representative and pretend to be a customer. During their discussion, she will obtain copy samples and learn as much as possible about product features, pricing, and marketing strategy. Lynn is hesitant about the ruse and doesn't want to waste the sales rep's time. However, Kyle insists that it is perfectly legal because no trade secrets will be stolen. People do this sort of thing all the time, and it is Hiyota's responsibility to make sure information doesn't leak out before the product hits the market. Besides, sales reps are accustomed to unproductive sales pitches, and who knows, the rep may convince Lynn to buy the new Hiyotas for her company.

## CASE 4.2

# A Damaged Car

### SYNOPSIS[3]

Joe was interested in buying a particular car at a dealership. He negotiated a price with the salesperson, Juan, along with a trade-in price for his old car. However, Joe had second thoughts, partly because the trade-in offer was below book value (i.e., below the published average price for a used car of that make and model). When he was about to walk away from the deal, Juan

gave him a lunch voucher for a restaurant a short drive from the dealership. He suggested that Joe have lunch and think it over. While at lunch Joe decided to buy the car, but he had a minor accident while driving back to the dealership. His old car suffered some body damage that was inconspicuous but significant. Joe guessed that the repair would cost at least $1,000. Yet he was almost certain that the people at the dealership wouldn't notice the damage, because they had already inspected the car. He decided not to mention the accident to Juan. It was only fair, because the trade-in offer was about $1,000 below book value.

## UTILITARIAN TEST

We can start with the utilitarian test because it seems to give Joe some support. Due to the concavity of utility curves, more utility would result if the dealer covered the cost of fixing the car than if Joe covered the cost or got less for his car. An amount of $1,000 is of little consequence to the wealthy dealer but a significant piece of change for Joe.

Joe admits that the dealer might pass the damaged car along to an unsuspecting buyer, in which case the buyer would have to pay for the damage. This could reduce utility because the buyer of a used car is likely to be less well off than Joe. But a utility increase is more likely, because it is more likely that the dealer would repair the car or give the buyer a price break because of the damage. So the *expected* utility is greater if Joe does not speak up. Joe's action therefore passes the utilitarian test.

## GENERALIZATION TEST

Breaking a sales agreement simply to save money is clearly ungeneralizable. If everyone broke sales agreements whenever it would save them money, agreements would lose their point, and there would be no sales agreements to break.

Joe might insist that he is not really breaking an agreement. He agreed to turn over his old car for a certain price, not in any particular condition. But this is clearly fallacious. Suppose the accident had been more serious, and a wrecker had towed his seriously damaged car to the dealership for trade-in. This would clearly be a breach of the agreement, because the car would not be in the same condition as when the deal was made. The actual damage is less serious, but the car is still not in the same condition, and the agreement is breached for the same reason.

Joe might also argue that I have drawn the scope too broadly. He is breaking the agreement in a particular way, namely by delivering damaged goods, and he has additional reasons for doing so. Not only will it save him money, but the damage was inconspicuous and happened after the deal was made. This makes his action generalizable. Inconspicuous damage between the deal and the delivery is rare. If customers never mentioned it, they would still be able to save money by not mentioning it.

This rationale for the action seems generalizable, but it is not Joe's rationale. Joe is willing to deliver the damaged car simply because the damage is inconspicuous. The time at which the damage occurred is irrelevant. But if people always followed a practice of delivering inconspicuously damaged goods, it would be equally standard practice for the buyer to check every delivery carefully. The practice is therefore not generalizable.

Joe defends his action on the grounds that he was offered a below-market price for the trade-in car. This is one of those arguments that sound convincing to someone who already agrees with the conclusion, but perhaps not to others. The relevant test for us is not whether the argument sounds convincing, but whether the action in question meets the conditions for rational choice.

We have already argued that Joe's action fails the generalization test because it breaks an agreement. The book value issue doesn't change this. Joe might regret making the deal because of the low trade-in price, but he nonetheless made it.

Joe might say that the low offer is one of his *reasons* for breaking the agreement, and this makes breaking the agreement generalizable. But it is one of his reasons only if he would be willing to mention the damage if he had been offered full book value. This seems unlikely. Even if he would, the action remains ungeneralizable. If sellers reneged on a deal whenever they thought the price was too low, deals would be meaningless. The whole point of a deal is that the seller has decided to deliver the promised goods at the agreed-upon price, be it high or low. A seller who is not satisfied with the price should not agree to it.

We can now evaluate Joe's decision:

1. Generalization test: *Fail*.
2. Utilitarian test: *Pass*.
3. Virtue ethics test: Not applied.

Joe is obligated to tell Juan about the accident. ■

## Exercises

7. It is argued above that returning a damaged car violates the sales agreement because the car is not in the same condition as when the agreement was made. Suppose Joe refutes this by pointing out that even if there had been no accident, he would not have returned the car in precisely the same condition. The few miles to the restaurant would put some wear and tear on the automobile, but no one would say that the agreement was breached. Thus the fact that the car is returned in an altered condition is insufficient to show that the agreement is breached. What is the flaw in this refutation?

8. There is a small chance that Juan will get in serious trouble with his boss when it is later discovered that the trade-in car is damaged. How might Joe argue that this does not affect the outcome of the utilitarian test?

**9.** Suppose Joe grants that if sellers always delivered damaged goods when the damage is inconspicuous, buyers would check carefully. But he, in particular, would still be able to deliver the damaged car, because the dealer would have already checked the car carefully and would not check again. Let's suppose Joe is right about this. Why does his action still fail the generalization test?

## CASE 4.3

# An Insurance Broker's Dilemma

### SYNOPSIS[4]

A major museum currently obtains insurance from Haverford, through its insurance broker Ashton & Ashton (A&A). It is time for renewal of the policy, and A&A has obtained several bids. There is one lowball bid from a "shaky" company called Reliable. If A&A conveys the Reliable bid to the museum, the museum will probably accept it. A&A receives 10–15% of the premium as commission, 17% in the case of Haverford. Should A&A present the low bid? If it does not, could it be accused of conflict of interest?

### ANALYSIS

It is helpful to view this as a case in professional ethics. It raises the question of what an insurance broker's professional duties are, with respect to conflict of interest and advising clients. As noted in Chapter 2, professional duties are based on the obligation to meet expectations that the profession created in the public mind.

The conflict of interest matter is easy to resolve. While professionals are normally expected to avoid or minimize conflicts of interest, the conflicts are often inherent in the nature of the profession. If so, professionals are expected to make the right decision without being influenced by personal incentives. In the present case, the conflict of interest is a built-in characteristic of insurance brokerage and exists whether or not A&A presents the low bid. It should have no bearing on how A&A decides to deal with its client.

The main issue is how many choices A&A should present to its client. There are two basic policies. One is to present the client a full range of representative bids, give advice, and let the client decide. A second policy is to make some decisions for the client by screening out bids that the broker thinks are clearly inappropriate.

As a rule, brokers are expected to give advice and not make decisions. This is not true of all professionals. Physicians, for example, generally present only the alternatives that they believe are medically sound. They may refuse to perform a surgery even when the patient requests it. If the surgery is medically ill-advised and turns out badly, the physician gets the blame. This is not inappropriate, because making this sort of judgment is part of a physician's professional promise. Public expectations appear to be evolving toward greater patient responsibility, but these expectations tend to be forgotten when a malpractice lawsuit is filed. Brokers, however, are generally expected to present the full range of alternatives, and the client is expected to take responsibility for the decision. Quoting the low bid is therefore consistent with professional ethics.

Furthermore, failing to quote the low bid seems inconsistent with professional duty. While a broker would not be expected to mention every option, it is important to provide a representative selection. One of the primary motivations for working through a broker is to make sure one is aware of the range of options. This may well reduce utility, because the museum is apparently unwilling or unable to make the right decision, even after hearing A&A's advice. Yet there is no obligation to achieve higher utility through actions that are otherwise unethical. A&A can be as emphatic and detailed as it wants, however, when it advises the museum to reject the lowest bid, and there is probably a utilitarian obligation to do so.

The primary virtues at stake are honesty and loyalty to the client. An honest presentation of the alternatives, together with a stern warning about the risks of insuring with Reliable, seems consistent with these virtues.

The action of presenting the low bid can now be evaluated:

1. Generalization test: *Pass.*
2. Utilitarian test: *Pass.*
3. Virtue ethics test: *Pass.*

The action is not only permissible but also obligatory, because failing to present the low bid fails the generalization test.

## Exercises

**10.** You engage a real estate "agent" (actually, broker) to help you find a house in an unfamiliar city and give her the price range. She only shows you houses that are at the upper end of the range, because her commission is a fixed percentage of the sales price. Does her conduct conform to professional ethics?

11. *Pricey insurance.*[5] Mark, an insurance salesman, is concerned about the product he sells most. It is a "whole" life policy that provides death benefits, retirement savings, and a fund that can be accessed in an emergency. The problem is that it is not a good deal for the young families who buy it from him. They would do better to buy a "term" life insurance policy, which provides only a death benefit, and use the savings to buy an annuity. On the other hand, term insurance and annuities are much less profitable for the company, and the sales commission is therefore much less. Mark's commission on a whole life policy is 110% of the first year's premium. Mark can support his family only by selling a substantial number of these policies. Is Mark living up to professional and other ethical obligations?

## CASE 4.4

# Product Safety

### SYNOPSIS[6]

For some years, Dow Corning manufactured breast implants designed for women who had undergone mastectomies. Testing was performed only on animals and provided no clear evidence that the implants would cause harm when properly used. Anecdotal evidence involving human patients, however, suggested that silicone oozing out of the implants could cause autoimmune reactions. The company sometimes told its salespeople to conceal the oozing by wiping the implants clean just before displaying them to surgeons. A court ruled the implants defective in a 1991 product liability suit. This gave rise to about 13,000 lawsuits, and in 1994, Dow Corning agreed to contribute $3.2 billion to a settlement fund. In 1995, the company filed for bankruptcy, from which it emerged only in 2004. In recent years, extensive studies have failed to confirm that silicon or any other design defect of the implants causes the autoimmune symptoms.

### THE ISSUE

The lawsuits against Dow Corning took place in the United States, where courts have enforced the doctrine of strict liability since the early 1960s. On this doctrine, a company must pay for damages caused by a defective product, no matter how hard it tried to make the product safe. Dow Corning may not have tried very hard, but this is legally irrelevant to product liability; the only question is whether the breast implants were defective.

The ethical question, however, is different. The company must decide when the product is safe enough to be put on the market. Too much caution and delay can be as harmful as too little, because they deprive patients of treatment. The fact that silicone now appears to be safe is irrelevant. What matters is whether Dow Corning acted ethically, given the state of knowledge at the time.

### UTILITARIAN TEST

The utilitarian principle seeks a schedule of testing and product releases that maximizes benefit and minimizes harm. The medical and regulatory communities have developed protocols with this aim in mind, and the utilitarian solution has probably been worked out as best can be done in the current state of the art. Dow Corning's duty, from a utilitarian point of view, was to follow best practices as they were known at the time. Given that only animal testing was carried out before the product release, it seems clear that the company fell short of its duty.

### GENERALIZATION TEST

There is no reason to believe that releasing a medical device that maximizes utility is ungeneralizable. However, an issue of distributive justice is at stake. It may be unfair to make a few women much worse off, even when this is offset by many women who are better off, and even when overall utility is maximized. We therefore apply the generalization test in the form of the Difference Principle.

The Difference Principle states that a policy should maximize the welfare of the least advantaged. On the face of it, a policy of providing breast implants appears to violate the principle. It doesn't maximize the welfare of the least fortunate, namely, those who suffer a rejection of the implant as well as a horrible disease. They would have been better off without the decision to sell implants.

Yet the Difference Principle pertains only to the smallest group that is controlled by the allocation, and not necessarily to individuals. In this case, Dow Corning can't control the reaction of individual patients to the implant. It can only control the welfare of the implant recipients in general. Because this group benefits on the average (assuming the implant maximizes utility), there is no violation of the Difference Principle. Even if they are the least healthy patients as a group after the implant, withholding the implant would have made them even worse off.

As for Dow Corning's conduct, the scorecard is as follows:

1. Generalization test:
   a. Basic test: *Pass.*
   b. Difference principle: *Pass.*
2. Utilitarian test: *Fail.*
3. Virtue ethics test: Not applied.

The company behaved unethically. ■

## Exercises

**12.** It is often said that if there is risk associated with a medical product, there should be full disclosure of that risk. Can you defend this claim using the conditions for rational choice, even when disclosure is not required by law?

**13.** A pharmaceutical company has developed a remarkably effective headache remedy and is deliberating whether to market it over the counter or as a prescription drug. Over-the-counter sales would be more profitable and would reach far more headache sufferers. However, the medication doesn't ease migraine headaches, the most severe type of headache. In fact, clinical trials suggest that for 10% of migraine sufferers, use of the medication results in twice as many headaches as before. The effect seems to be permanent, or at least to last as long as the trials. An over-the-counter label could carry a warning to migraine sufferers, but many of them don't realize that their headaches are migraines. If the drug required a prescription, doctors would dispense it only to patients without migraines. Would over-the-counter sales satisfy the Difference Principle? *Hint.* There are two groups to compare when applying the Difference Principle: those with severe cases and those with mild cases.

**14.** A new flu medication can act as a cure or as a vaccine, but a curative dose is 10 times larger than a vaccination. The cure and the vaccine always work. Half of healthy persons who don't receive the vaccine will get the flu. The medication is in short supply. Health authorities can use all of it as a cure or all as vaccine, or some combination of the two. What allocation maximizes utility? What allocation(s) satisfies the Difference Principle? *Hint.* Utility is measured by the number of persons who don't get the flu. There are potentially four groups to consider when applying the Difference Principle: treated sick patients, untreated sick patients, vaccinated healthy patients, and unvaccinated healthy patients. The benefit to a group can be measured by the probability that a person in that group will get the flu.

**15.** In the previous exercise, suppose that the vaccine works only half the time. What allocation maximizes utility? What allocation(s) satisfies the Difference Principle?

**16.** A million persons nationwide have a chronic disease. A thousand of them have a rare, severe form of the disease that is fatal, and the rest have a mild form that gives them a headache once a week. A new bioengineered drug can cure a mild case or convert a severe case to a mild case. The drug is hard to manufacture and in short supply, and a severe case requires very large doses. There is enough to treat all the severe cases or all the mild cases, but not both. How should the drug be allocated to satisfy Rawlsian ethics?

**17.** In the previous exercise, suppose that severe cases are not fatal but only cause headaches twice a week. Everything else is the same. What is the ethical allocation? *Hint.* Examples such as this one suggest that a purely Rawlsian allocation may be inappropriate when the utilitarian cost is too high. This is an active research issue in ethics, particularly in the health area.

## CASE 4.5

# Misleading Numbers

**SYNOPSIS**[7]

I was confronted with an ethical dilemma firsthand in a previous job as a financial advisor. One of my tasks was to prepare a report to clients. In a one-on-one meeting, a manager asked me to exclude certain past performance numbers for one of our mutual funds, because they greatly lagged behind our stated benchmark.

All marketing literature published in the investment advisory industry has a footnote, "Past performance is not an indication of future returns." Theoretically this is true, but past performance influences both investors seeking investment products and consultants who recommend investments. In this particular instance, I was not instructed to change the numbers, which would be a blatant ethical violation, but rather to exclude data for a product with historically poor performance.

Although no law required companies to show all relevant product performance records to a client, it was extremely misleading to exclude this poor performer from the group that was shown. The manager seemed to only be concerned about increasing the assets under our management and not accurately representing our past investment performance, or about the ethical issue. As is often the case, this manager was more concerned with increasing shareholder value than our duty to clients. Should I tell the manager that I cannot comply with this request?

## DECEPTION

This is the most common sort of ethical dilemma described by my students: The boss asks them to do something questionable. There are two issues in such cases. Is the requested action ethical in itself, and if not, does one have an obligation to defy the boss?

The first issue is relatively easy in the present case. Although every statement in the report will be true, the report will nonetheless be deceptive. To deceive is to cause someone to believe something you know is false. Omitting information is not always deceptive, but in this case it is, because it causes readers to believe mistakenly that the bank's asset management is uniformly successful. This is the whole point of omitting the bad numbers. If there were no desire to deceive, the bank would have no objection to adding a note to the title page: "This report omits all bad news."

Deception merely to benefit oneself is ungeneralizable. This is because deception serves this purpose only if people believe the deception, and they would not believe it if people were routinely deceptive. Deception continues to be ungeneralizable when the scope is narrowed to the context of a financial report to clients. A report can mislead clients only if it has credibility. If companies regularly left out the bad numbers, clients would throw such reports in the trash.

As for the matter of shareholder value, we noted in Chapter 2 that while board members and top executives have a fiduciary responsibility to owners, the primary duty of other employees is to follow the instructions of superiors. The issue therefore reduces to whether there is an obligation to obey the boss in a case of this sort, and fiduciary duty is irrelevant. This is precisely the second issue stated above.

## THE PRICE OF BEING ETHICAL

How high a price must you pay to be ethical? There is a clearly a limit. If the boss is holding a gun to your head, you don't worry about such trifles as omitting numbers from a report. But if there is a limit, what is the limit? Must you risk your job, for instance?

It is not as though the boss will fire you on the spot, because this would require the boss to justify the action. Note that in the case description, the boss's request was delivered orally and in private. Rather than outright dismissal, your next performance review will be lukewarm, resulting in your being passed over for promotion, or your inclusion in the next reduction in force.

There is another consideration. *If you don't do it, someone else will.* The boss will find someone else to do his bidding and reward that person with promotions and salary raises. The impact on the clients will be the same.

The question, "How high a price must you pay to be ethical," may give the wrong impression. It may suggest that ethics tells you that it is unethical to mislead clients, whereupon you must decide what to do about it. Ethics is not finished until it tells you whether to obey the boss. Once you decide whether it is ethical to obey the boss, it makes no sense to agonize further about what you "should" do. The ethical choice is, by definition, the one you should make.

## UTILITARIAN TEST

In practical situations you may instinctively try to defuse the situation. Perhaps you can avoid a stark choice between dishonesty and defying the boss. You might try to reason with the boss or suggest a compromise solution that reports the bad numbers but (honestly) points out the extent to which they are misleading. By all means, do so. This kind of compromise maximizes utility while avoiding unethical behavior.

If the boss insists on having his way, however, you can apply the utilitarian test to the either/or situation before you. Unfortunately, the consequences are hard to evaluate for either option. Defying the boss could hamper your career and make it more difficult for you to make useful contributions in the future. If you lose your job, it could result in financial difficulties for you and your dependents. On the other hand, your boss may forget about the whole thing, or even respect you for your courage.

As for obeying the boss, it could compromise your reputation for honesty and, again, prevent you from making valuable contributions in the future. One act of dishonesty can have very damaging effects on an individual, because people generally assume that anyone who is willing to be dishonest once will do so again. On the other hand, the whole affair may go unnoticed. Finally, omitting the bad numbers may induce your clients to make unwise investments.

How about the argument that if you don't do it, someone else will? Actually, we don't know that someone else will. Yet we should think about how to deal with this kind of response, because it comes up so frequently. One can imagine security personnel who are ordered to murder political prisoners saying to themselves, "If I don't do it, someone else will." Is this a valid argument?

Assuming that someone else will really do it, this may be a valid *utilitarian* argument. It may show that refusing will have no effect on utility, which means that the act may pass the utilitarian test. However, this doesn't show it meets the other conditions for rational choice. Murder, for example, is the most extreme denial of autonomy and thus unethical on that ground alone.

In the case of the misleading numbers, the utilitarian test is inconclusive, which means that either choice passes it. The other conditions for rational choice must now be brought to bear.

### GENERALIZATION TEST

Identifying the reasons for omitting the numbers is crucial to the analysis. Deception simply to benefit yourself is ungeneralizable, but perhaps the additional factors at play in this case reverse the judgment. One obvious reason is to benefit your career by obeying the boss. If this were the only reason, the action seems not only generalizable but in some historical contexts already generalized. It is not hard to think of times and places in which subordinates regularly did what they were told, however odious it might have been, to benefit their careers—and they continued to benefit their careers by doing so.

Because the action in question is not simply to obey the boss, but to do so by deceiving customers, the issue arises as to whether the deception is one of the reasons for your action. You might think that it is not, because your interest is in obeying the boss, not in deception. You would obey the boss whether or not the deception succeeded. The issue is important, because obedience is probably not generalizable if you must deceive to accomplish your purpose. If employees were always willing to deceive for their bosses, then bosses would probably require deception often enough that the deception would no longer be effective.

It's clear, however, that you must deceive to accomplish your purpose. Your aim is to protect your career by obeying the boss, and the boss wants the clients to be deceived. If you omitted the numbers but sent all the clients an e-mail warning them about the omission, then your boss would not be satisfied.

It remains to explain why you wouldn't be obligated to disobey the boss if he held a gun to your head or there were some other very serious consequences. It is because the argument against generalizability breaks down. If all employees deceived simply to avoid the vague threat of negative career consequences, then bosses would take advantage of this, and attempts to deceive would be rampant. But this would not occur if employees deceived only under serious threat. Even now, nearly all employees are willing to deceive under a sufficiently dire threat, and bosses rarely respond by issuing such threats.

### VIRTUE ETHICS

Misleading clients violates integrity whenever it occurs, both because it is dishonorable in itself and because it is contrary to the mission of this employee's profession. You are a financial advisor, the essence of which is to help clients make the right investments. Misleading clients is the precise opposite. The boss, who hired you to be a financial advisor, is asking you not to be an advisor. The inconsistency is clear enough. Virtue ethics clearly requires you to remain honest, unless there is another virtue at stake.

There may in fact be another virtue at stake if you have heavy family obligations. Perhaps your elderly parents require very expensive care or your child is disabled and requires constant therapy. In this case, the virtue test is harder to evaluate; you must do a balancing act and decide whether family loyalty is more important than personal integrity.

If serious family burdens are your only reason for obeying the boss, however, you can rerun the generalization test. In fact, serious repercussions for your family are another form of serious consequences if you don't obey. So the argument against generalizability breaks down as above.

In summary, a decision to obey the boss stacks up as follows:

1. Generalization test: *Fail*, unless your family situation carries extraordinary financial obligations.
2. Utilitarian test: Inconclusive, and therefore *Pass*.
3. Virtue ethics test: *Fail*, unless perhaps your family situation carries extraordinary financial obligations. ▩

## Exercises

18. Suppose the boss compromises and allows you to describe the list of performance results as a "sample" of results (it is, after all, a sample consisting of all but one). Does this change the analysis?
19. Suppose the boss compromises some more and allows you to report only the *average* performance of the funds. Does this change the analysis?

## CASE 4.6

# Health and Smoking Bans

### SYNOPSIS[8]

Ford Meter Box Company has a total nonsmoking policy, not only at work but at home as well. The policy is enforced by requiring employees to submit to periodic blood tests to check for the presence of nicotine. The rationale for the policy is that smokers cost the company substantially more in health care bills and days off. However, some employees have objected to this intrusion into their personal lives, and a few have brought suit.

### THE ISSUE

This case involves both a privacy issue (the nicotine test) and a personal freedom issue (the smoking ban). We will focus on freedom issue.

Strict rules against smoking on the job have become commonplace and accepted in the United States, largely on the grounds that secondhand smoke endangers the health of nonsmokers. However, the secondhand smoke argument does not obviously support an after-hours ban, since smokers can be careful not to endanger others. The ban at Ford Meter Box rests solely on a cost-saving argument. For the sake of distinguishing this issue from the privacy issue, we will suppose for the moment that it is obvious whether one smokes during after-hours (it creates bad breath, or whatever), and no blood test or other invasion of privacy is needed.

### UTILITARIAN TEST

There is an obvious slippery-slope argument against the smoking ban. If companies ban smoking today, then tomorrow they will refuse to employ individuals who are overweight, have cancer in the family, pursue dangerous hobbies, show a genetic propensity to diabetes, and so forth. Before you know it, most of us will be unemployable, and this is not a utilitarian outcome.

There are two problems with this argument. One is that slippery-slope arguments are rarely backed up by convincing evidence that the slope is in fact slippery, and that is the case here. The other is that a slippery slope, even when it exists, is irrelevant to the utilitarian test. The test is not whether utility is maximized when companies in general reject employees with health risks. The test is whether utility is greater when Ford Meter Box in particular bans smoking than when it does not. It is hard to argue that a smoking ban at this one company reduces utility, because some employees may, after all, stop smoking and improve their health as a result. The utilitarian test must therefore be judged as inconclusive.

### GENERALIZATION TEST

The generalization test looks at the reason for the no-smoking policy: It reduces costs. But if this is a reason to exclude smokers from the workforce, then it is a reason to exclude all workers with detectable health hazards that increase costs. This is not a slippery-slope argument, because the generalization test does not assume that this and other companies will in fact exclude all employees with expensive health conditions. It only asks whether it would still be possible to cut costs if they did.

It probably would not. If every company tried to externalize health care costs in this way, the government or society in general would have to pick up a much greater burden. After all, few of us have perfect bodies, and someone must pay the costs of illness. Taxes and social costs would be much higher (think of Sweden), and Ford Meter Box would end up paying the cost anyway through taxes and otherwise. The only reason the company can externalize the costs now is that other companies carry their share of the load. It is therefore unethical for Ford to make an exception for itself by trying to reduce its share of health care costs below the norm.

A common reaction to this conclusion is that it is permissible to ban *voluntary* behavior that creates a health risk. This sounds like a more reasonable policy, but a reasonable sound does not prove anything. Let's apply the generalization test. We suppose that the company ban extends only to smoking, illegal drug use, and other clearly voluntary and dangerous activities that incur significant health-related costs. This policy seems generalizable on the face of it, because if adopted by all companies, the population in general would be obliged to adopt healthier habits and actually reduce the social costs of illness.

The fact remains, however, that a smoking ban is a restriction of personal freedom that many would find objectionable. Is there a rational basis for their objection? One might construct a generalization argument on a cultural level. A company that does business in a particular culture relies on that culture for the institutions and practices that make its business possible. It should not act to undermine the culture, because such an action is not generalizable. Perhaps the availability of a certain range of lifestyle choices is an essential element of Western or U.S. culture and should be respected on that basis. We will explore this type of argument in the last chapter of the book.

### LIBERTY PRINCIPLE

A smoking ban restricts freedom and might therefore run afoul of the Liberty Principle. Ford Meter Box is likely to respond that there is no restriction of freedom, because no one is forced to work for them. This response is not helpful, however, because if a smoking ban is justified at Ford Meter Box because it cuts costs, then it is justified at any company where it would cut costs, which is to say, nearly all companies. So the policy in question effectively denies employees the freedom to smoke.

Employees can argue for a violation of the Liberty Principle on the ground that a ban on smoking and similar behavior restricts basic liberty unnecessarily. The ban is necessary only to spare others the social costs that result when some people smoke. To make this argument go through, employees must argue that a smoking ban restricts a basic liberty, while requiring others to bear the costs of this habit does not.

We have not provided a complete analysis of the case, but this discussion indicates some directions in which the analysis might go. To sum up, we can distinguish two types of policies the company might adopt. One is to exclude all employees with major health risks, which scores as follows:

1. Generalization test: *Fail.*
2. Utilitarian test: Inconclusive, and therefore *Pass.*
3. Virtue ethics test: Not applied.

A broad policy of this sort is unethical. A more restrictive policy is to exclude employees who pursue voluntary behavior that incurs major health risks. The scorecard is as follows:

1. Generalization test:
   a. Basic test: *Pass* in an initial analysis, but further study needed.
   b. Liberty Principle: Possible violation.
2. Utilitarian test: Inconclusive, and therefore *Pass.*
3. Virtue ethics test: Not applied.

This is a difficult issue that requires further analysis. ▪

## Exercises

20. *On sale next week.*[9] Bernie walks into an electronics store and tells Sam, the salesman, that he is looking for a particular model of flat-screen TV. The model is in stock and will in fact go on sale for 15% off the following week. However, Sam does not mention the upcoming sale to Bernie, because Sam's commission would be proportionately less. Is this ethical?

21. *Cheap stuffing.*[10] Elite Furniture Manufacturing has a reputation for high-quality upholstered furniture. Hard economic times have hit, however, and the company must cut costs quickly. Top management orders that from now on, an inferior grade of padding will be used in the upholstery, on the expectation that customers won't notice the change at the time of purchase. Is this an ethical decision?

22. *Uncrushable Volvos.*[11] At a monster truck rally in Vermont, a huge "Bear Foot" truck drove over the roofs of several cars and crushed all but a Volvo. Volvo's advertising agency recreated this scene for a highly acclaimed television commercial. Engineering analysis confirms that the Volvo is strong enough to support the truck, and the other cars are not. However, the agency reinforced the Volvo and partially sawed through the roof supports of the other cars. The agency claimed that this was necessary for production purposes. The State of Texas sued Volvo for consumer fraud based on deceptive advertising. Is it deceptive advertising, in the sense that it misleads customers about the product? Is it deceptive in some other way? Can the ad be altered in some small way to make sure it is not deceptive?

23. *Delayed delivery.*[12] Don is production scheduler at Fitzgerald Machine Company, where a large order is scheduled to go out Friday. The customer calls, however, and asks Don to delay the delivery at least a week beyond Friday, due to a labor dispute at the customer's plant. On authorization from his boss, Don complies with the request on the condition that the customer will remit the amount due Friday, as specified in the original contract. The customer agrees to these terms, and Fitzgerald sends a bill payable Friday. The next day, Don learns from the production manager that the order won't be ready until at least a week beyond Friday. Don does not mention this to the customer and collects the payment Friday as agreed. Is this deceptive? Is it ethical?

24. *Taking credit.*[13] Janice is Chief of Research and Development. Her boss asked her some time ago to design software that would solve certain problems at the company, but she has been too busy to think about it. However, her assistant John invents a creative solution on his own initiative and shares it with Janice, in hope of boosting his meager salary. Janice is impressed by his proposal and tells John that she is going to take credit for the idea. If he objects, she will downgrade his performance evaluation, but if he cooperates, she will give him a promotion and a substantial raise. Is her action ethical?

25. *Poor morale.*[14] Stacy graduated near the top of his business school class and takes a job at a growing CPA firm. Despite his ability and training, Stacy finds himself unable to deal with several assignments. He gradually learns that there has been heavy turnover at the senior level, and as a result he is assigned tasks that require a more experienced accountant. He begins to receive reprimands for his blunders, one delivered loudly in front of coworkers. The firm eventually hires a psychologist to interview staff and determine the reason for growing turnover at all levels. The staff complain of poor working conditions and low morale. When the partners read the psychologist's negative report, they take it personally, and there are rumors they will put the firm up for sale. Nonetheless, the firm continues to interview for its vacant staff positions. The partners ask all those who are interviewing candidates to present the firm in a positive and favorable manner. Stacy is unsure how candid he should be with his interviewees.

26. *A pizza puzzle.*[15] Sharon is Restaurant and Food Services Manager for Marigold Inn. She is concerned about a decline in room service orders, the highest margin portion of her operation. After some marketing research, she concludes that guests are ordering pizzas from outside the hotel because they cannot believe a hotel restaurant can make an authentic pizza. She therefore proposes the following to George, General Manager of the inn. She will put Napoli Pizza brochures in the rooms, with a phone number having a different prefix than the hotel number. Calls to this number will reach a special phone in room service, which will be answered, "Napoli Pizza, authentic Italian pizza from old, family recipes." Hotel personnel will don a "Napoli Pizza" hat and coat when delivering the pizza in boxes marked "Napoli Pizza." The hotel chef, Luigi, will in fact make the pizzas according to an old family recipe. How should George respond to this proposal? If it is unethical, how can the plan be modified to make it ethical?

27. *Unmentioned plans.*[16] It is October, and Boris is in his third year at a large accounting firm. He finds the job less than satisfactory due to his heavy workload. He therefore applies for several MBA programs and expects to enroll in one of them next fall. Meanwhile, a firm partner in charge of staff development, Julie, tells him about five-month internships at the firm's overseas offices. The requirements for the assignment include language fluency and long-term career potential at the firm. Julie says she can probably get him the assignment at the Moscow office due to his fluency in Russian. Boris is excited about the opportunity because he has relatives in the Moscow area. He decides not to tell Julie about his MBA plans.

28. *The incredible shrinking potato chip package.*[17] Julie is brand manager for potato chips. Due to an abrupt rise in the price of potatoes, she must raise the unit price 15% to maintain the already-slim margins. She hits on the idea of reducing the package contents 13% but retaining the current price. This would result in the same revenue as before if unit sales don't change. She suspects that customers who would balk at a higher price won't notice that the bag is slightly less full. Her boss assures her that "package shorting" is standard practice in the industry and may well have the intended effect. It is also legal, because the package will indicate the correct net weight. The boss leaves the decision to Julie, and she must decide whether package shorting is a deceptive practice.

29. *Better is good enough.*[18] Kirk is being groomed for the controller's position in a medium-sized manufacturing firm. While attending a monthly financial meeting, he listens intently as the company's chief engineer explains that the firm's new plant, now on the drawing board, will require an upgrade of the current waste disposal system if it is to meet industry standards. However, the existing facilities are in compliance with minimum legal requirements, even if some environmental activists are pressuring the government for tougher standards. Bob, company president, points out that the closest competitor in the business has waste treatment facilities that are even inferior to theirs. He is therefore not in favor of further expenditures in this area. Most managers at the meeting express strong agreement, and the discussion moves to another topic. Kirk soon begins reflecting on whether this is the right firm for him. *Hint:* First analyze the president's decision, and then Kirk's personal decision.

30. *Another type of discrimination.*[19] Paula is Brand Manager for a line of soap used to scrub floors. Her assistant Terry is uneasy about the fact that Paula's plan calls for advertising spots that feature unattractive actors. In her view, this kind of ad promotes harmful stereotyping of less-attractive people. Paula defends her plan by citing an article in a top marketing journal, which reports research showing that sales are enhanced when attractive people appear in ads for glamorous products and unattractive

people appear in cooking and cleaning ads. Terry, however, carried out a project in college in which she reviewed over 1,000 studies of societal attitudes toward physical appearance. She found a strong bias against unattractive people, who are discriminated against in employment and education even when equally qualified. Can she make an ethical case against Paula's advertising plan?

**31.** *Whistle-blower accepts a deal.*[20] An auditor employed by a pharmaceutical company submitted documentation to the Food and Drug Administration (FDA) to support the approval of new drugs. He later suspected inaccuracies in the information he provided for one particular drug and, upon investigation, discovered that the project director in fact falsified data. When he reported this to his superiors, the company board of directors offered the auditor a deal. If he will not interfere with the FDA's imminent decision to approve the drug, the company will discontinue the drug and request the FDA to withdraw approval due to "mistakes in marketing projections." The aim was to avoid the bad press that would result from public knowledge of the falsification. The auditor accepted the deal, the company kept its word, and the project director quietly resigned. No further scandals of this sort have occurred. Was the auditor's decision ethical?

**32.** *Family plans.*[21] Barbara has been with Apex for four years and is now controller. Apex will merge with another firm on July 1, two weeks from now, and the ensuing staff cuts will be announced on August 1. The new company will need only one controller. Barbara hears through the grapevine that Sam, controller at the other company, is perceived favorably by management but will probably be dismissed, perhaps because he has been at the firm less than a year. In the meantime, Barbara has dealt with the increasing burden of caring for her parents. Her father has cancer and is expected to live six months. Her mother needs frequent support. In addition, Barbara is expecting her first child in a few months. She plans to take a short maternity leave and return to work. She believes that she can balance her personal and professional life, but she wonders if she should make her boss aware of her situation before August 1.

## Notes

1. Based on Case 6.3, "Procter and Gamble Goes Dumpster Diving," in John Boatwright, *Ethics and the Conduct of Business*, 4th ed., Prentice-Hall, 2003, pp. 151–152, and on Julian E. Barnes, "P&G placed under monitor in spy case," *New York Times*, September 1, 2001, p. C-1.

2. Based on the Arthur Andersen mini-case *I Spy: A Case of Competitive Espionage* by Nancy Artz.

3. This case was provided by an MBA student. The names are fictitious.

4. Based on Case 6.2, "Conflict of an insurance broker," in Boatwright 2003, pp. 150–151.

5. Based on the Arthur Andersen mini-case *Life Insurance: Who Benefits, the Consumer or the Company?* by Thomas W. Bose.

6. Based on Case 11.1, "Dow Corning's breast implants," in Boatwright 2003, p. 273, and subsequent news reports.

7. This case was contributed by an MBA student. The student's description of the case is quoted almost verbatim.

8. Based on Case 7.3, "Ford Meter Box," in Boatwright 2003, pp. 180–181.

9. Based on the Arthur Andersen mini-case *The Speedy Sale* by Geoffrey P. Lantos.

10. Based on the Arthur Andersen mini-case *Elite Furniture* by David J. Fritzsche.

11. Based on Case 11.2, "Volvo's 'Bear Foot' misstep," in Boatwright, pp. 303–304.

12. Based on the Arthur Andersen mini-case *The Fitzgerald Machine Company* by Eliot S. Miner and William Roth.

13. Based on the Arthur Andersen mini-case *Might Makes Right* by J. H. Coll.

14. Based on the Arthur Andersen mini-case *Psych Me Out* by Curtis J. Bonk and Mary M. Bonk.

15. Based on the Arthur Andersen mini-case *The Pizza Puzzle* by Fred L. Miller.

16. Based on the Arthur Andersen mini-case *To Go or Not to Go* by Cynthia L. Rooney and Mary Loyland.

17. Based on the Arthur Andersen mini-case *The Incredible Shrinking Potato Chip Package* by Geoffrey P. Lantos.

18. Based on the Arthur Andersen mini-case *Safety? What Safety?* by G. Stevenson Smith and Curtis Jay Bonk.

19. Based on the Arthur Andersen mini-case *Another Type of Discrimination* by Gordon L. Patzer.

20. Based on Case 5.2, "A Whistle-Blower Accepts a 'Deal,'" in Boatwright, pp. 120–121.

21. Based on the Arthur Andersen mini-case *Family Plans* by Cynthia J. Rooney and Mary Loyland.

# Chapter 5

# MBA Student Dilemmas

This chapter analyzes ethical dilemmas experienced by MBA students. All of the dilemmas were provided anonymously by my students, except the last, which is based on a published case study. I edited the student write-ups lightly for clarity but changed none of the facts. Names and other identifying information are, of course, altered to preserve anonymity. Almost all of the cases describe personal dilemmas on the job or in everyday life, as opposed to company policy decisions, presumably because these students typically have only a few years' work experience and have not risen high enough in the company to influence policy. The next chapter focuses on broader issues faced by organizations.

All of the case studies that appear in exercises describe ethical dilemmas faced by my MBA students or professionals in executive workshops I have facilitated.

## CASE 5.1

## Being Honest with the Customer

Prior to entering business school, I was a salesman for a small aerospace and defense contractor. My role was to sell our software and consulting services to the government and other contractors. On several occasions, I knew that our software could not perform all the functions a prospective customer needed, and I was faced with the dilemma of whether to be honest about this. Because I was responsible for 20–25% of company revenue, it was absolutely essential that I meet quotas. The company's normal response to low revenue numbers was to lay off employees, no doubt including me. One particular dilemma involved a major sale that, if completed, would allow me to make my quota for the year and pay for my first semester of business school. I therefore led my customers to believe that our software could meet their needs.

### INITIAL ANALYSIS

When viewed from a distance, the case seems clear. You are deceiving the potential customer by misrepresenting the capabilities of the software. Deception is ungeneralizable, even in the specific case of salespeople. The reason you want to mislead the customer is to generate more revenue. If all salespeople were deceptive when it would generate more revenue, then they would have absolutely no credibility, and it would be impossible for them to generate revenue by deception.

However, the situation may not seem so clear when it is up close and personal. In a perfect world, you would love to confess all to the customer. But do you have the right to sacrifice jobs, and perhaps even a company, for the sake of your personal scruples? After all, salespeople are not expected to point out the negative side of a product. You need a solid analysis that you, and ideally others, find convincing.

### UTILITARIAN ANALYSIS

Part of your thinking suggests a utilitarian perspective. Failure to make the sale could cost jobs, including your own, which is a very negative outcome. On the other hand, the short-term cost is at least partially offset by the long-term damage to the company that can result from dissatisfied customers. A client that is stuck with inadequate software may have to compromise its operations or pay technical staff to find a work-around, which again reduces total utility.

You can probably make an educated guess about the net utilitarian effect of dishonesty. For the sake of argument, let's suppose you decide it is positive. Given sufficient revenue now, the company will at some point upgrade the software, take care of its customers, and mitigate the reputational damage. If it loses big sales now, however, none of this can happen. This means that you have a utility-based obligation to make the sale, unless deception fails other tests for rational choice. We now turn to this question.

### GENERALIZATION TEST

You deceive a customer if you cause the customer to believe something you know is false. Thus you need not tell an outright lie to deceive. You need not say literally that the software will meet all customer needs. It is enough that you lead the customer to believe as much. But deception for the purpose of increasing revenue is ungeneralizable, as already pointed out.

You might argue that you are deceptive not merely to boost revenue, but specifically to save jobs. You would never mislead a customer simply for the sake of profitability. This narrows the scope of the rationale, but it remains ungeneralizable. If salespeople always deceived when jobs are potentially at stake, then customers of a small firm like yours would be on the alert, particularly big customers who can substantially impact the firm's cash flow. They would insist on technical evaluation, trial periods, contractual penalties for nonperformance, and so forth.

You suggest that your presentation of the product is not really deceptive because salespeople are expected to gloss over the negative. The customer allows for this already and is not deceived. This is true in some contexts. However, if your customer makes allowance for "sales talk" about the capabilities of the software, then your dishonesty will have no effect on the sale. The customer will evaluate the software by other means. This is an interesting scenario to analyze, but it is clear from the case description that you believe your deception will have an effect. To be consistent, you must recognize that your intent is deceptive and therefore ungeneralizable.

### VIRTUE ETHICS

The virtue of loyalty is potentially at play in this case. There is, for example, your loyalty to your customers. If you have worked with client representatives over a period of time and developed a relationship, particularly one that implies mutual trust, then loyalty requires you to care about them. Because loyalty applies to human beings, not companies, it doesn't matter how long you have worked with a particular company. What matters is your relationship with individuals representing the company. The case description provides no evidence that such a relationship exists, however. If so, loyalty to the customer has no bearing on the analysis.

There is also the matter of loyalty to coworkers whose jobs may be at stake. If you have developed a bond with them, as sometimes happens in the business world (particularly in small firms), you have an obligation to care about them as well. Again, loyalty in this sense is not owed to the company, but to human beings. The case description is unclear as to whether you enjoy this kind of relationship, but to make the situation more interesting we can suppose that you do.

The next question is whether loyalty entails an obligation to deceive. We determined in Chapter 2 that virtue ethics should be clarified by, rather than override, the generalization principle. It is in fact unclear, solely from a virtue ethics perspective, whether loyalty to coworkers requires going so far as to deceive customers. The generalization principle tells us that it does not.

We can evaluate your deception as follows:
1. Generalization test: *Fail*
2. Utilitarian test: *Pass*
3. Virtue ethics test: *Pass*

---

## Exercises

1. You can still ask whether deceiving the customer is generalizable if loyalty to coworkers is one of your reasons for being deceptive. What is the answer?
2. Suppose your customers study the software and conclude that it is adequate for their purposes. You know better, because you are more familiar with problems that arise after installation. However, you say nothing about this, and the customers continue to believe that the software is adequate. Is your silence ethical?

## CASE 5.2

# Paying for the Salad Bar

## SYNOPSIS

At a school cafeteria where I sometimes eat, customers pay the cashier for meals as they leave. Employees come by the tables and write up a bill that indicates the plates selected. I sometimes opt for the soup and salad bar. The price for one trip to the bar is $4, and for unlimited trips it is $5.75. On one occasion, I made two trips, but as I paid for the meal I realized that the bill indicated only one trip. I didn't know what to do. I thought about how the tuition rate had just been raised at this already very expensive institution. I also reasoned that most people would pay $4 even if they made two trips to the salad bar, and this was already reflected in the cafeteria prices. If so, then I would have been a chump to pay. Yet, I did go to the salad bar twice.

## INITIAL ARGUMENTS

There is not a great deal at stake in this dilemma, but small issues can provide good practice in ethical reasoning. At first glance, the case appears straightforward. You understand how the cafeteria operates. By patronizing it, you agree to abide by the terms of sale, which specify a payment of $5.75 for two trips to the salad bar. Breaking sales agreements merely to save money is obviously ungeneralizable, as noted in Case 4.2.

You make a couple of remarks in defense of paying the lower rate. You first observe that the university charges a great deal for tuition. This might be interpreted as a utilitarian argument. Due to the concavity of utility curves, the $1.75 surcharge would presumably create more utility in your possession than in university coffers. Whether this is true depends on how university funds are distributed, but it is irrelevant in any event, because it is neither permissible nor obligatory to increase utility by violating generalizability.

There is also a suggestion in your remark that by paying high tuition bills, you are "already paying for" the extra salad. This is simply false. The tuition payment may be excessive, but it is in exchange for educational services, not food.

You claim that most people who pay $4 make two trips to the salad bar, and this is factored into the price. Assertions that "most people do it" tend to be based on surmise rather than evidence, but let's suppose you have evidence for this. Presumably this is "factored into" the $4 price in the sense that customers who are billed for one trip consume $4 worth of salad *on the average*. The cafeteria can therefore recoup its costs by charging $4. It is unclear how you know this, but again we will suppose you have reason to believe it. But what does it prove? It is not as though you pay for two trips by handing over $4, because $4 reflects only the cost to the cafeteria of the average customer who pays for one trip, not the customer who actually makes two trips.

## GENERALIZATION TEST

We might interpret your remarks as an argument that paying $4 passes the generalization test. The reasons for paying $4 for two trips are presumably that it saves money and that the cafeteria billed you for only one trip. You might argue that if everyone who could save money in this fashion did so, the reasons for doing so would still apply, because the cafeteria would not raise the one-trip price further as a result. But why not? After generalization, *all* customers are making two trips. Because the cost of two trips is $5.75, the cafeteria can recoup the cost only by charging everyone $5.75.

You might argue that the cafeteria would retain the $4 price because the managers would be unaware that everyone is making two trips. Yet you claim they are now aware that *most* people are making two trips. Why would their observational powers degrade if customer appetites increased? You have no apparent reason to believe they would. (Recall that the generalization test is based on what is rational for you to believe about the consequences of generalization, not what the consequences would actually be.) Your rationale for underpaying therefore fails the generalization test.

1. Generalization test: *Fail*
2. Utilitarian test: *Further study needed*
3. Virtue ethics test: *Not applied* ▣

## Exercises

3. You buy a number of expensive items at a store. On arriving home and looking over the itemized receipt, you realize that the cashier forgot to ring up a Sony DCR-HC46 MiniDV Digital Camcorder with Optical Zoom, which retails for $599.95. What should you do?

4. Suppose that in the previous exercise, the cashier forgot to ring up a 50¢ pack of gum rather than the camcorder. What should you do? Why should the value of the item make a difference? *Hint.* Sales agreements can be modified with mutual consent.

## CASE 5.3

# The Boss's Unauthorized Expenses

### SYNOPSIS

My boss asked me to accompany him on a business trip to San Francisco. I agreed and asked the company travel agent to make my reservation, charging it to my boss's account. While confirming the transaction, the agent noticed that my boss had booked a third person for the trip. When I asked her who it was, I recognized the name of my boss's wife (who uses a different surname than my boss). My boss was charging the company for all of his wife's personal expenses. Should I report this to the company, speak to my boss, or ignore it?

### THE BOSS'S CONDUCT

The first task is to determine whether your boss did something wrong. If he did, then we can ask whether you should take some kind of action.

The boss's conduct is clearly unethical. It is deceptive, because he led the company to believe that the third party was a business traveler. For reasons already discussed, deception for personal benefit is ungeneralizable. It also violates the boss's promise to abide by company rules, a promise he made (explicitly or implicitly) when he took the job. This is again ungeneralizable. The issue before us, then, is whether you should report the boss's unethical behavior or at least talk to him about it.

### UTILITARIAN ANALYSIS

The utilitarian fallout of reporting the boss is hard to assess. This is a minor case of (internal) whistle-blowing, and the consequences of blowing the whistle are notoriously hard to predict. Reporting the boss could wreck your career while having no perceptible effect on the company, or it could expose a widespread practice, thus improving the company and making you a hero. We will have to view both reporting and not reporting the boss as passing the utilitarian test, because there is no clear evidence that either results in more expected utility than the other.

### GENERALIZATION TEST

Some may say that employees have a duty to report irregularities, even when they involve the boss. We can check this by asking whether a failure to report is generalizable. Presumably, one reason for not reporting is that you want to pursue a successful career without risking retaliation. Suppose employees never reported fraud against their company when their careers could be at risk, including auditors and other employees who are charged with monitoring the books. This would make it much easier to get away with fraudulent behavior, perhaps to the point that business success would be more difficult to achieve. A less-successful business could jeopardize your career, thus defeating the purpose of your action.

However, we may assume that an important element in your decision is that you have no specific responsibility to report irregularities. If only those employees with no such responsibility failed to report minor infractions, then arguably company auditing mechanisms would still work well enough to allow you to pursue your career. At least, there is no clear reason to believe otherwise. Your failure to report therefore seems generalizable, assuming that you would be willing to report your boss if it were your specific responsibility to do so.

The picture could change if you witnessed a major accounting irregularity. Business scandals over the last decade or so have taught us that such misconduct not only threatens a company's existence but can occur unchecked for surprisingly long periods when managers fail to blow the whistle—including managers whom the company has assigned no specific duty to report fraud. Thus if you witnessed serious misconduct, you would have to rethink your obligations.

The situation may involve an element of virtue ethics, because you may have a loyalty obligation to your boss, depending on the relationship you have developed. However, this would only provide an additional reason not to report him.

To sum up our assessment of a failure to report:
1. Generalization test: *Pass*
2. Utilitarian test: Inconclusive, and therefore *Pass*
3. Virtue ethics test: *Pass*

A failure to talk with your boss about the situation would probably receive a similar assessment. ▪

---

## Exercises

5. Suppose your boss invites you to bring your wife along at company expense. What should you do?
6. Suppose the travel agent asks you who the third party is. What should you say?
7. *No oversight at the brokerage.* I was a retail stockbroker working on a team that catered to high net worth speculative investors. One night I had some spare time, so when our team risk report arrived, I decided

I could do a favor for the teammate who normally signed off on risk reports and take care of it myself. I was astonished to find that she had not done any oversight for weeks. As a result, we had been in violation of New York Stock Exchange regulations for quite a while, and dozens of client accounts were illegally overextended. Three accounts had no equity left, and our firm was stuck with hundreds of thousands of dollars of customer losses. My teammate had signed off on all of the daily risk reports, attesting to our accounts being in good standing. This was a shock, given that we were a tight-knit group. The problem had to be corrected, but I didn't want to be the one to expose it. Revealing the lapses would embitter my manager and teammates and perhaps invite reprisals. It would do nothing for my advancement and would poison the collegial atmosphere of our team. I wanted to look the other way and let someone else discover the problem. Did I have an obligation to speak up? *Hint*: How does this case differ from?

8. *Reporting cheaters.* While an undergraduate student I witnessed three friends cheating on an exam. If caught, they would be expelled from school, which could bar them from finding a good job or getting into another school. They were smart, and the exam was relatively easy, but they cheated nonetheless. Should I have turned them during the exam or just let it pass and talk to them about it later?

9. In the previous exercise, would it make a difference if the penalty for cheating were milder?

## CASE 5.4

# Accepting Free Tickets

A representative from of my company's suppliers invited my girlfriend and me to join him at a hockey game. It is common for suppliers to entertain employees on occasion, with the expectation that they will "talk shop" during the engagement. The representative gave me the tickets, and my girlfriend and I were to meet him and his wife at the game that evening. While we were on our way to the game, the representative rang my mobile phone to say that he could not make it due to a personal problem. He told us to go ahead and enjoy the game and take full advantage of the club level to which the tickets entitled us. So, we watched the game. This wasn't unethical, was it?

## ANALYSIS

Attending the game clearly satisfies the utilitarian test. Your decision affects only you and your girlfriend (the tickets are not refundable), and it is better to enjoy the game than waste the tickets.

However, the situation seems to imply a kind of agreement, and breaking an agreement is normally ungeneralizable. The supplier gave you the tickets on the understanding that you will listen to his sales pitch. Because the supplier won't be at the game, you are not sure you should use the tickets.

You might argue that the representative released you from the agreement when he told you to go ahead and enjoy the game. This could be true if he has the authority to release you on behalf of his company, which is paying for the tickets.

Even if you are not released from the agreement, your obligation under it is to listen to the sales talk. Whether the representative watches the game or not is irrelevant. Perhaps you have an obligation to hear out the vendor at a later time, but this is another matter.

Some may object that accepting this sort of gift from potential suppliers is a violation of professional ethics. Although you have already accepted the tickets, *using* the tickets could likewise violate professional ethics if such a practice creates an appearance that purchasing agents are influenced by conflicts of interest. The case description suggests, however, that accepting occasional free entertainment is consistent with industry practice and would therefore presumably meet the expectations of stockholders and other interested parties. This may or may not be true, but if it is, and if the practice does not interfere with good business judgment, then there is no breach of professional ethics.

Virtue ethics does not seem relevant in this case. It is therefore ethical to use the tickets—unless, of course, you are so burdened with uncertainty over the issue that you can't enjoy yourself, in which case watching the game violates the utilitarian test. However, your ability to apply the conditions of rational choice should avoid this problem.

1. Generalization test: *Pass*
2. Utilitarian test: *Pass*
3. Virtue ethics test: *Not applied* ∎

## Exercises

**10.** Suppose the supplier representative phones you a couple of days before the game to say that he can't make it, but he will have his company purchase the tickets for you and your girlfriend. Is it ethical for you to accept the tickets? Why would the timing of the ticket purchase make a difference?

**11.** Suppose you have already made a long-term contract with a competing supplier, and there is no chance you will source from the supplier who invites you to the game. Yet he is unaware of this, and he phones you a couple of days before the game to invite you and your girlfriend. You reveal the situation, but he tells you not to worry about it. The company has already bought the tickets, and he and his wife would like to enjoy the game with you. Should you and your girlfriend go along?

---

### C A S E   5 . 5

# Unauthorized Salary Information

#### SYNOPSIS

At one point in my previous job I came up for a performance review, which included discussion of my salary. While searching the company's HR intranet site to download the annual review form, I came across a file containing salary and benefit information for almost every employee in the company. I viewed the file purely by accident and broke no company rules by accessing it. The HR department, which is responsible for maintaining the confidentiality of such information, had mistakenly placed the file in an unprotected area. The data revealed that I was receiving a considerably lower salary than my peers, many of whom held less responsibility. Should I use the salary information in my annual review?

#### CONFIDENTIALITY

Violating confidentiality for personal benefit is ungeneralizable, at least when the benefit depends on the fact that the information is confidential. If people violated confidentiality at will, confidentiality would no longer exist, and the information would provide no benefit. However, you can use the salary information without violating confidentiality. You can make your point by referring only to salary levels already known to your boss. Furthermore, the usefulness of the information does not depend on the fact that it is confidential.

You must nonetheless apply the generalization test to your situation. We can suppose your reasons for using the information are that it may help you negotiate a better salary, you came across the information accidentally, and you won't violate confidentiality by using it. Could you still achieve your purpose if everyone who came across confidential information under these circumstances made use of it? There is no clear reason why not, particularly because accidental discoveries of this kind are rare. The action is generalizable.

Nothing in the case description suggests that using the information would reduce overall utility. It passes the utilitarian test.

You may have loyalty obligations to your coworkers. However, it is hard to maintain that negotiating an equitable salary would violate loyalty obligations, particularly when your coworkers already have higher salaries than you do.

We can now evaluate your proposal to use the information in your salary negotiations:

**1.** Generalization test: *Pass*
**2.** Utilitarian test: *Pass*
**3.** Virtue ethics test: *Pass* ▪

---

## Exercises

**12.** If you decided not to use the salary information for negotiation, would you nonetheless have an obligation to tell the company you discovered it?

**13.** A free online news service requires users to register by proving certain information, such as address, gender, age, and salary bracket. The Web site promises that the information will remain confidential. Despite this promise, the news service provides the information to some of its advertisers, with no strings attached. Is this policy generalizable?

14. Suppose a sealed note is mistakenly placed in your office mailbox. You open it and start reading before you realize it is addressed to your coworker Brad, who is married with three kids. It is a passionate message from a lover in another division of the company with whom Brad is having an affair. They evidently exchange love notes through company mail. Is it OK, or even obligatory, to inform his wife about this? Don't just say, "Of course not, it's none of my business." Provide an argument based on the conditions for rational choice.

15. *A revealing plant visit.* I visited a manufacturer's facility to investigate its ability to scale up our manufacturing process for widgets. We didn't sign a confidentiality agreement before entering the plant. During the tour, we passed a production line that manufactured gadgets for a competitor. Gadgets are unrelated to widgets, but the competitor had long undersold us on gadgets, and we had been trying to reduce our manufacturing costs. The representative who was showing us around was unaware that this company was our competitor and proceeded to tell us all about the gadget product line and its performance level. Should I have stopped him?

## CASE 5.6

# Sacrificing the Old for the New

### SYNOPSIS

I work for a small company that designs software for financial institutions. We have the potential to attract a new client that is much larger and more profitable to the company than any of our present clients. However, if we take on this new client, we will have to provide a substantially lower level of service to our other clients, because our entire workforce will be preoccupied with projects for the new client. Due to the complexity of the software, hiring more people won't resolve the issue in the short term. If we drop everything and start working for the new client, we will lose some established clients that played a major role in the development of the company. The choice is between attracting the new client and maintaining our relationship with the existing ones. We can't have it both ways.

### WHY THIS CASE IS HARD

It is interesting to think about why we find this an uncomfortable choice and why we are so keen to find the middle ground that you insist is not an option. For one thing, it may be a tough business decision. There is risk in alienating established clients for the sake of a glamorous new client that may drop you like a hot potato in a year. Another reason may be that you feel that you "owe something" to the established clients that helped you build the firm, and you are unsure whether such obligations should be sacrificed to hard-nosed business considerations. We will deal with the latter issue first by applying a generalization test. The former issue is related to the more general question of which choice maximizes utility, which will be the deciding factor for this case.

Before proceeding, we should clarify that this is not your decision to make. It is a company decision and therefore a decision that is ultimately taken by the owners of the company (which we will call SmallSoft). Nonetheless, we can address the issue of what the owners should do.

### GENERALIZATION TEST

Let's assume, as the case description seems to imply, that SmallSoft can drop or neglect existing clients without violating its contractual obligations. The company would simply decline to renew existing contracts. Nonetheless, the clients could maintain that there is an implied agreement that is ethically, if not legally, binding. They might say, "We made a commitment to you by building our businesses around your software. We expect a similar commitment to us."

However, it is normal practice in the business world to be clear about commitments of this kind, normally by writing them in contracts. It is hard to see how the small clients can reasonably claim that SmallSoft promised to keep them as clients beyond the term of the current contract, unless such a commitment was discussed orally or clearly implied in the conversation. It is therefore hard to ground an obligation on an implied agreement.

We can also apply a generalization test directly to the action of abandoning clients. Suppose that companies always abandoned existing clients (legally) when they thought they could grow their business by doing so. Would they still be able to grow their business by doing so? It is hard to see why they would not.

There could also be a question of loyalty to clients. As always, the kind of loyalty that counts for our purposes is loyalty to human beings. Even if you have developed personal relationships with client representatives that would call for loyalty, what matters is whether the owners have such relationships, because they make the decision. It seems unlikely that they have.

SmallSoft therefore does not "owe" its existing clients a continued business relationship. This is not because hard-nosed business considerations are more important than feelings. We are not trying to balance business with feelings. Rather, we are applying the generalization test, and we find that it does not establish an obligation in this particular case.

## UTILITARIAN TEST

It is important to distinguish the business decision from the utilitarian decision, if the business decision is understood as concerned solely with the welfare of the firm. This is not because the business decision is irrelevant to a utilitarian assessment. It is very relevant, because if SmallSoft suffers, this not only creates disutility in itself but also hampers the firm from making positive contributions in the future. Nonetheless, the utilitarian calculus must consider the whole picture.

Abandoning existing clients could cause them significant damage. Unable to obtain continued maintenance, they may have to retool for different software, perhaps at considerable expense. If abandonment is also a poor business decision for SmallSoft, because the risk creates negative net expected utility for the firm, then the utilitarian verdict is clear: Don't do it. However, if abandoning small customers is good for SmallSoft and bad for them, then the choice becomes harder.

You might want to argue that by taking on a major new client, SmallSoft will grow and create enough value to outweigh any loss experienced by the abandoned clients. However, even if this is true, it alone does not make the case. If SmallSoft fails to grow and provide valuable services to many clients, probably some other firm will provide these same services and reap the same rewards. The net utility created could be the same. To make your case, you must show that SmallSoft would provide significantly more valuable service than competitors, valuable enough to outweigh the loss to your present clients.

Thus, if SmallSoft has a truly unique contribution to make, you may have a case. But if not, and if abandoning its current clients would cause substantial harm, SmallSoft must take care if its clients first. This may seem perverse, because the overriding imperative in the business world is to grow and prosper. However, utilitarianism tells us that the ultimate purpose of rational business owners must be to make the world better off, not worse off. If growth at the present time would cause net harm over the long run, it must wait.

To sum up the permissibility of abandoning present clients:

1. Generalization test: *Pass*
2. Utilitarian test: *Pass*, unless (a) abandoning clients is a poor business decision for SmallSoft in the long term, or (b) it is a good business decision, but abandoning present clients would cause them harm that outweighs any services that only SmallSoft can provide after accepting the new client.
3. Virtue ethics test: *Pass* ■

## Exercise

16. The above analysis rests on the assumption that there is no implied promise to continue servicing clients past the legal period of the contract (unless such a promise is made orally). However, our analysis of Jennifer's job decision claims that there is an implied promise to work longer than the two-week notice period. Why are the two situations different? *Hint.* Under what conditions would the agreements involved lose their point?

## CASE 5.7

# Interviews after Accepting a Job

SYNOPSIS[1]

After an initial campus interview, MBA student Mike Anderson traveled to New York City for an on-site interview with the leading investment banking firm Morgan Baker Aldrich Inc. Shortly afterward, he interviewed in San Francisco with a second firm, McClaren Manufacturing.

Both firms offered Mike a job. John Thayer at Morgan Baker Aldrich (MBA) made the first offer and asked for a response within two weeks. Two days later, McClaren offered Mike a position as assistant to the vice president for finance. However, McClaren insisted on an answer within five days, despite Mike's request for more time. This created a problem for Mike, because his girlfriend was also looking for a job, and there was not enough time for her to

investigate job opportunities in New York City. Rather than lose the McClaren offer, Mike accepted it as the deadline was about to expire.

Five days later, Thayer called Mike from New York City to ask about his decision. Mike said that he was still thinking about it, without mentioning that he had signed with McClaren. Thayer invited him and his girlfriend to New York for a second visit and showed him some parts of the city where they might live. She interviewed with a company there as well.

After a few days, Mike turned down Thayer's offer on the grounds that his girlfriend didn't want to live in New York City. But as it happened the two companies had a long-standing relationship, and Thayer learned through the grapevine about Mike's dealings with McClaren. He asked Mike why he visited New York a second time when he had already accepted a job offer in San Francisco. Mike replied that he was prepared to renege on the McClaren offer if he preferred the MBA offer.

Three weeks later, Mike sent Thayer a $6,200 bill for reimbursement of expenses incurred on his two trips to New York City.

## THE ETHICAL ISSUES

Two issues stand out. One is whether it was ethical for Mike to visit Morgan Baker Aldrich after having already signed with McClaren. The second is whether Thayer should reimburse his expenses.

Neither question is as easy as it may seem. A theme of this case is the pressure created by the competitive market for MBAs. Mike might argue that although he would not ordinarily continue to interview after signing, McClaren put undue pressure on him. By making an unreasonable demand on the response time, the company forfeited its right to a commitment from Mike. If it is unwilling to treat Mike fairly, it should not expect fair treatment in return.

As for the expense claim, Mike can insist that he acted in good faith with Thayer all along, because he was willing to renege on his McClaren contract if he preferred Thayer's offer. As far as Thayer is concerned, the situation is precisely what it would have been if Mike had not signed with anyone else. Thayer therefore has no reason to reject the expense claim.

These arguments are likely to sound convincing to some and not to others, and nothing is resolved. To make some progress, let's apply the conditions of rational choice.

## THE NEW YORK INTERVIEW—UTILITARIAN TEST

The question is whether Mike should continue to interview in New York City after having committed to McClaren. Let's first apply the utilitarian test.

The utilitarian test requires Mike to select the option that maximizes utility while passing the other tests for rational choice. So it is OK, in fact obligatory, for him to continue talking with Morgan Baker Aldrich if doing so maximizes expected utility and passes the other tests. This is what makes the case hard. Without the utilitarian argument, Mike could just tell Thayer that he had already signed with McClaren, and that would be the end of it. This would allow him to come clean with both companies and honor his contract.

Many people would say Mike should do just that. He should simply come clean and honor the contract. These people say that ethics is simple. Just do what your mother would tell you to do. The hard part is not figuring out what to do, but doing it.

There are certainly cases in which the right action is obvious and doing it is hard. But it can be equally hard to tell what is right. It isn't clear what Mike should do, and perhaps even less clear what his mother would tell him to do! "Coming clean" and keeping the McClaren contract could cause Mike and his girlfriend to pass up New York jobs in which they would make substantial contributions

to their companies and to society. It would be irrational, and therefore unethical, to turn down better jobs when there is no obligation to turn them down. So it is important to know whether Mike really has an obligation to honor the contract with McClaren.

The case description is vague on exactly why Mike wants to keep pursuing the New York job. To make the case interesting, let's suppose that it is because he sees a possibility that he and his girlfriend could make substantially greater contributions in New York. But they can't really tell without further investigation. So the *expected* utility for all concerned is probably greater if they obtain more information. As it happened, they would have made the same decision with or without the additional information, but they didn't know this in advance.

Naturally, Mike's duplicity with Thayer could create problems, and this must be factored into the expected utilities. It could establish a bad reputation for Mike, which would not only reduce his own utility but make it hard to realize his full potential as a contributor to society. Thayer might refuse to hire Mike anyway if he learns about Mike's dealings with McClaren.[2] These are serious considerations, but again to make the case interesting, I will assume that the potential advantages of the New York jobs outweigh these risks in a utilitarian calculation.

None of this is meant to imply that the *only* potential problem with Mike's conduct is its effect on his reputation. His behavior could be unethical for other reasons. Nonetheless, reputation must be considered in a utilitarian analysis.

## THE NEW YORK INTERVIEW—GENERALIZATION TEST

Let's move on to the generalization test. We can begin by observing that Mike never actually broke his contract with McClaren. However, when he interviewed a second time, it was his *intention* to break the contract if he liked the New York job better. Otherwise there would be no point in talking further to Thayer. It is the intention that makes the act what it is.

Mike's intention is ungeneralizable, because if everyone kept interviewing after signing, the employment agreement would lose its point. New hires would honor the agreement only if they don't find a better job, which they would do without an agreement. So employers wouldn't bother to promise a job, and Mike would have no agreement to break. So Mike has an obligation to honor his employment agreement and to stop looking around.

Mike can argue, however, that there is actually no agreement (at least form an ethical point of view), because there is no mutual consent. Mutual consent means that both parties freely chose to enter into the agreement. This is why a legal contract signed under duress is often considered void. In this case, the pressure comes in the form of a tight deadline. One might argue that the agreement is nonbinding because Mike was given too little time for deliberation. U.S. consumer law recognizes this principle when it allows customers to cancel a purchase from a door-to-door salesperson within three days.[3]

Adequate deliberation is a condition for free action, because without it, we cannot adequately explain the action as based on a coherent rationale. It is the existence of such an explanation that distinguishes free action from mere behavior. If Mike's signature was not the result of free action, then there was no mutual consent.

To sharpen the argument, let's suppose for the moment that McClaren demanded a decision by the end of the day (rather than within five days). Given the circumstances surrounding Mike and his girlfriend, there is no way he could make a rational choice so quickly. Perhaps it would be unethical for him to decide on impulse in the first place, because an ethical choice must be a rational choice. But whether he should have signed is not the issue here. It is too late to think about that. The issue is whether his signature binds him to an agreement, and arguably it does not, because there was no mutual consent.

Even if Mike can escape his agreement, perhaps he is still unethical, due to deception. He is not telling McClaren about his second interview in New York, because if he does, McClaren may withdraw its offer. Perhaps this is deceptive, and deception merely for convenience is ungeneralizable.

Mike can respond that he didn't actually cause anyone at McClaren to believe that he has made up his mind. They know that Mike can't make a rational job decision on the spot. Perhaps they impose tight deadlines on the chance that some people will be gullible enough to take them seriously, but with full knowledge that others will keep looking. If so, then Mike's silence about his New York interview didn't cause them to believe that he had made up his mind.

Things are different if the McClaren people gave Mike a plausible reason for requiring a fast response. Perhaps their second-choice employee gave them a deadline before she takes a job elsewhere, and the deadline is today. Then Mike's silence could genuinely lead them to believe that he has made up his mind, and it is therefore deceptive not to tell them he is still looking.

Do these arguments apply when the time limit is five days? With a longer time limit, they are less compelling. But we have established the principle that excessive pressure in the form of a tight deadline can make an employment agreement voidable, at least from an ethical point of view. If the agreement is still binding legally, and McClaren refuses to release Mike from the contract, then this may change the picture. Illegal behavior is normally unethical, because it is ungeneralizable. But I will assume that McClaren is willing to release Mike from all legal obligation if it comes to that.

Excessive pressure can also relieve Mike of the obligation to tell McClaren what he is doing, but this depends on what Mike knows about McClaren and its reasons for imposing a tight deadline.

I would like to wrap up the argument here, but there is more. Even if Mike is not ethically bound by a contract with mutual consent, and even if there is no deception, he may nonetheless have an obligation to honor what McClaren *thought* was an agreement. Contract law recognizes this principle in the idea of a quasi-contract. Suppose, for example, that someone knocks on your door

and offers to shovel the snow off your walk, and you say, "Sure, please do." A little while later he knocks on your door and asks for $10. Your response: "Oh, you want to be *paid* for this!" Legally, there may be a quasi-contract, which means you may owe him $10 even though there was no mutual consent.

Let's use the generalization test to see if this idea applies in Mike's case. Suppose everyone who hastily agrees to employment continues to look around, with the intention of taking a better offer if it materializes. The purpose is to find a better job, if possible, while retaining the security of the first offer. It is hard to say that Mike would be unable to achieve this purpose if everyone behaved similarly. Although employment agreements would lose their point if offered when the deadlines are tight, employers might continue to make meaningful offers by avoiding tight deadlines. Then Mike would still be able to look around while retaining the security of an offer, because McClaren would give him more time. We can't be sure that employers would respond in this way, but we don't have to be sure. We only have to establish that it is consistent with Mike's belief system that they would continue to offer contracts. So Mike has no ethical duty to stick with the McClaren job.

## THE REIMBURSEMENT

The utilitarian test is of little relevance to the reimbursement issue. Reimbursing Mike may increase total utility somewhat, because the owners of Morgan Baker Aldrich are likely to be wealthier than Mike. The concavity of utility functions implies that a transfer from richer to poorer results in a net increase in utility. But it is clearly ungeneralizable to disperse company money simply because it increases net utility. Otherwise managers would donate all their stockholders' money to starving peasants around the world, nobody would invest in companies, and there would be no companies to donate.

Presumably, the basis for reimbursing Mike is an agreement between the company and Mike. If the company has a general practice of reimbursing interviewees, then there is an implied agreement that the company will cover Mike's expenses in exchange for his continued interest. Normally, it is ungeneralizable to break an agreement simply to save money. So Thayer would normally have an obligation to reimburse the cost.

In this case, however, Mike's willingness to interview again, without mentioning that he had already accepted a job, clearly misled Thayer about his circumstances. This would ordinarily void the agreement because it implies lack of mutual consent as to the terms of the agreement. When Thayer invites Mike for a second interview, it is because he believes there is a certain probability that Mike will accept his offer. His assessment is based on Mike's situation, including the presumption that Mike has not already accepted a job. Mike is therefore deceiving Thayer as to what he is getting in this agreement.

Mike, however, insists that his prior acceptance has absolutely no effect on the probability of his accepting Thayer's offer. If this is really true, it means that Thayer's probability assessment is correct after all. For this reason, and for this reason only, the agreement is valid, and Thayer owes Mike the reimbursement.

Thayer might respond that the (implied) agreement is void because he was misled about Mike's *character*. He would not have asked Mike for a second interview if he had known about Mike's duplicity. Because an agreement requires mutual consent, deception about the consideration (i.e., what is exchanged under the agreement) can void the agreement. But Thayer's consideration is an interview with Mike, not Mike's services as an employee. More precisely, it is an interview with a candidate having Mike's resume who is available for employment. If the resume falsified Mike's background, Thayer could claim failure of consideration, but we will presume the resume was accurate. Thayer might not have arranged the interview if he had known more about Mike, but this is often the case with interviews. The purpose of the interview is to learn more about the candidate. So it is hard to make a case that Mike's duplicity voids the interview agreement.

None of this says that it is ethical for Mike to deceive Thayer about his situation. It only says that the deception does not void the reimbursement agreement. Mike's lack of candor is an ethical issue in its own right that we should address. The argument of the previous section established that, under certain conditions, it is OK to interview a second time in New York, but it did not establish that it is OK for Mike to interview *and* fail to mention his acceptance of the McClaren offer.

Mike's failure to mention his job acceptance is clearly deceptive. When Mike accepts Thayer's offer of a second interview, Thayer will infer that Mike has not signed with anyone else. Deception is ungeneralizable when achieving its purpose depends on the fact that the other party is in fact deceived. In this case, the purpose is clear. Mike doesn't want Thayer to get ticked off when he learns that Mike is double-dealing, because he might cancel the interview and rescind the job offer. If it were not so, Mike would be willing to reveal the McClaren commitment up front. The deception must therefore work to achieve Mike's purpose.

Thus, even if it is OK for Mike to interview a second time, he must mention the McClaren job when accepting the invitation to interview. Mike can of course reassure Thayer that he will renege on the McClaren commitment if he likes Thayer's offer, and he can describe the haste with which he was required to respond to McClaren. Thayer may rescind his offer when he hears all this, but this is a chance Mike must take.

## CONCLUSION

The ethical obligations of job applicants can change if employers apply unreasonable pressure. If McClaren demands very fast response from Mike—by the end of the day, for example—then Mike has no binding agreement with McClaren, from an ethical point of view, provided McClaren would be willing to release Mike from legal obligations if he reneged. Nor is there any reason to treat this as a quasi-contract that, despite the lack of mutual consent, imposes an obligation on Mike to honor it.

It is therefore ethical for Mike to make a second trip to New York, if he sees a possibility that he and his girlfriend could make substantially greater contributions there, and a second visit would help resolve the matter as well as result in greater expected utility. However, it would not result in greater expected utility if there is a significant chance that a second visit would create a bad reputation for Mike or cause Thayer to withdraw his offer. In this event, the second visit is unethical on purely utilitarian grounds.

Mike has no obligation to tell McClaren that he is still considering the New York job, unless he has some reason to believe that the people at McClaren would be genuinely surprised, despite their tight deadline, to learn that he has not yet made up his mind.

However, Mike must tell Thayer about his situation at McClaren when he accepts Thayer's invitation for a second interview, even though this may induce Thayer to withdraw his job offer. To avoid this risk, Mike would have to go back to McClaren and tell them that he is declining their offer so that he can pursue an opportunity in New York City.

Because Mike's deadline is five days rather than the close of business today, the arguments in favor of a second visit become much weaker. They remain valid only if Mike had no time to make a deliberate and rational choice in five days, and perhaps he did. Nonetheless, we have established that unreasonably tight deadlines can, at least in principle, relieve job applicants of some contractual obligations, and this is the primary issue raised by the case.

If Mike's commitment to McClaren has absolutely no effect on the probability that he would accept a job from Thayer, then Thayer has an obligation to cover Mike's expenses—even if Mike fails to mention that he has signed with another company.

To sum up the ethics of the second New York interview:

1. Generalization test: *Pass*, if Mike had only a short time to give McClaren an answer. The pass is clear for a one-day deadline, but less clear for five days. However, Mile must tell Thayer about the McClaren job when he accepts the invitation for a second interview, and take the risk that Thayer will withdraw his job offer.
2. Utilitarian test: *Pass*, if the expected utility of Mike's career contribution is significantly greater in New York City before his second visit, and there is no significant probability that the second visit would create a bad reputation for Mike or cause Thayer to withdraw the job offer.
3. Virtue ethics test: Not applied.

None of this implies that it was OK for Mike to sign with McClaren before he was ready. It was probably unethical, but we did not address this issue because it was a done deed. ▨

# Exercises

**17.** *Filching printer paper.* When I take business school classes, I prefer to have a hard copy of the notes that are distributed electronically by the professors. Because there is typically a long line of students at the school printer, I print my notes at home. This not only makes better use of my time but reduces ink consumption and wear and tear on the school printer. However, class notes require a great deal of printer paper, and I would like to take home a pack of the paper that is stockpiled near the school printer. I would use it only for printing class notes. Given that I would consume the same paper if I printed the material at school, is there an ethical problem with this?

**18.** *Vacation allowance.* My previous employer allowed 10 vacation days a year, which could be used at any time without management approval. In addition there were five personal days, for which there were very specific restrictions. They could be used only to take care of a sick child, attend a funeral, or complete the sale of real estate. My boss, however, told me to use personal days as though they were vacation days. In fact, he said I should use personal days first, because they could not be rolled over from year to year as vacation days could. Was it OK to follow his advice?

**19.** *Unqualified intern.* While a systems engineer at a bank, at one point I shared a cubicle with Michael, a summer intern. I got to know him quite well, and we became friends. Near the end of the summer, I learned from my supervisor that he was going to recommend Michael for a permanent position. I was naturally happy for Michael, but disconcerted at the same time. Over the summer I had learned that Michael didn't have the ability for the job. In fact, I had to assist him with his internship duties several times over the summer. Should I have informed my supervisor that Michael was unqualified?

**20.** *Playing someone else's shell game.* I was working as a contractor for a company that had several concurrent projects with the same client. Each project had a budget, and some had more money left in the budget than others. The company would face a penalty for each budget it exceeded, and it would collect a bonus whenever it came in under budget. While I was working on project A, the company asked me to charge some of my expenses to project B.

**21.** *Too much sophistication.* I was a relatively new associate in the sales and trading division of a major investment bank. One of our tasks was to value and manage risk for structured securities, which can be a very complicated affair. My particular job was to help prepare materials used by a sales force that sells less-risky securities to such traditional investors as insurance companies, pension funds, and fixed-income mutual funds. Riskier securities were sold to hedge funds. At one point I realized that a relatively obscure valuation approach commonly used for another product could help traditional investors understand specific types of risk associated with their investments. I wrote some materials to describe the approach, but my director told me not to share them with the sales force. He said that he didn't want traditional investors to start viewing their securities in this way. It would complicate the sales process and make it harder to create demand for new deals. However, I thought we owed it to our clients to provide a more sophisticated risk valuation method. *Hint.* Note that this case concerns a company decision, rather than the decision of this individual.

**22.** *Fraud in Armenia.* I was a Peace Corps volunteer in a small Armenian mining town. I spent a year trying to learn the language and local customs, and in the process I got to know the owner of a local poultry farm. Aside from the mine, this farm was the largest employer in town, with roughly 300 employees, although many of them worked only part time due to bad management. I estimated that if the farm were managed properly, it could employ another 300. I began meeting with the farm's accountant and discovered that he owned a computer, at which point I began to teach him to use Excel. After a time he began to realize the value of what I was teaching, and he stopped his heavy drinking before and during our sessions. Although there was plausible deniability, I got the strong impression that he wanted to prepare multiple sets of books: one for under-the-table investors in the United States, one for the relatively corrupt Armenian government, and a true version for resource management. I concluded that if I taught him enough to upgrade the poultry operation, he would use the same knowledge to commit fraud. Should I discontinue my efforts?

23. *Blaming the subcontractor.* I worked for EPI, a contractor that specialized in the construction of manufacturing plants. EPI does most of its own work but subcontracts for electrical and instrumentation systems. Engineers at EPI prepare the drawings, estimate the required hardware, and issue subcontracts to the most competitive bidder. The subcontractor, generally a small company, orders the hardware three or four months in advance, because of long lead times. It then completes the construction under the supervision of EPI engineers. Upon reaching the construction site, I found that the installation drawings were wrong, and as a result the subcontractor had not procured some of the hardware. I reported this to George, top boss at the site, who instructed me to correct the drawings and hand over a list of additional hardware items to the subcontractor's foreman. I was to tell the foreman that these items should have been ordered by the subcontractor. George explained that I must make it appear that the items were included in the initial hardware list, so that EPI could avoid paying the hefty cost (about $70,000) of expedited delivery of these items. In other words, George wanted me to cover up EPI's mistake and get the subcontractor to pay the additional cost. *Hint.* First evaluate George's action and then address the decision his subordinate must make.

24. *Inside information?* Mr. Martin was, until recently, head of investor relations at Verband, a Fortune 500 company. He had risen steadily through company ranks, due to his infallible judgment and ability to tell the company story in a most marvelous way. This was not an easy task, as Verband had a habit of covering up its blunders. The company had major discrepancies in its accounts and, in particular, lied to stockholders over the years about the lack of progress in its overseas operations. However, Martin was adept at putting the company in the best light while diverting attention from any discrepancies. The private banking division at EuroBank, however, had been scrutinizing Verband carefully on behalf of its clients. The research team contacted Martin numerous times with penetrating questions, which he always skillfully deflected. The research team was so impressed that they recommended that EuroBank try to hire Martin. Due to a very generous offer and rumors that Verband was looking for a buyer, Martin transferred to EuroBank. He quickly became as successful as he had been at Verband. On one occasion, the head of private banking offered a wealthy client with large holdings in Verband a presentation by a former Verband insider, who of course was Martin. Martin prepared the presentation carefully so as to use only data in the public domain to reveal the serious discrepancies in Verband's statements. Revelation of anything more would have violated his contractual confidentiality obligations to Verband. The difference between Martin and any other analyst is that, as a former insider, he knew exactly where to look for the discrepancies. Following the presentation and a series of follow-up meetings with Verband management, the client sold his large holdings, causing the share price to plummet. Verband was subsequently taken over at a much reduced price. Martin and his colleagues at EuroBank are convinced that his presentation to the client was entirely proper. After all, Martin's judgment is infallible.

---

## Notes

1. Based on the case study *Arthur Johnson* by John P. Kotter, Harvard Case 9-483-064, 1996. The case begins with a letter from an executive at fictitious firm Morgan Baker Aldrich to a business school dean who is given the name Arthur Johnson in the case. The letter expresses concern over unethical recruiting practices and includes a description of Mike Anderson's dilemma. My thanks to David Krackhardt for suggesting this case.

2. As it happens, Thayer did learn about Mike's duplicity through personal contacts at McClaren. Although this is not mentioned in the case, Thayer reportedly stated that he would have refused to hire Mike because he didn't want an employee he couldn't trust. Hiring Mike would also have created friction between MBA and McClaren, a valued client, because McClaren would have regarded MBA as stealing an employee. But it is too easy to resolve the issue by pointing to these facts. If Mike knew them it would obviously have tipped the utilitarian balance, but he didn't know them.

3. *16 CFR Part 429.*

# Chapter 6

# Business Case Studies

Most of the case studies discussed in this chapter have been used by my business school colleagues for teaching purposes. The cases were assigned reading in accounting, econometrics, marketing, operations management, organizational behavior, and strategy courses. The instructors discerned ethical issues in the cases and suggested to me that an ethical analysis may be beneficial.

The analysis is often more complicated than in previous chapters, due to the complexity of the cases. At the end of the chapter are several additional exercises that present case summaries and ask for an ethical analysis, using guidelines suggested in the exercise.

## CASE 6.1

## Nortel and Income Smoothing

### SYNOPSIS[1]

Nortel Networks was a telecommunications company based in Toronto, Canada. During the period 2000–2003, some of its executives relied on income smoothing to help meet quarterly income targets. This is the practice of transferring income expected in the next quarter to the present quarter, to bring reported income up to par. The executives feared that if the company came in below its target, the market would punish it with a lower stock price.

One of Nortel's primary tactics was the questionable use of bill-and-hold transactions. This is a transaction in which the customer orders a product in the current period but does not take delivery until next period. U.S. Generally Accepted Accounting Principles (GAAP) allow the seller to recognize the revenue from the sale in the current period, if certain strict guidelines are met. One of these is that the buyer must initiate a request for the bill-and-hold transaction and must have a substantial business purpose for doing so.

To create the appearance that it met this condition, Nortel offered several customers incentives to write letters requesting bill-and-hold transactions. The incentives included price discounts, interest deferments, and extended billing terms.

### REVENUE MANAGEMENT

Nortel is using *revenue management*, a euphemism for manipulating the books to make revenue or profit appear in certain periods rather than others. The most common type of revenue management is *income smoothing*, which is the issue here. Income smoothing evens out the fluctuations in profit or revenue from one period to the next. Various motivations are cited for this practice. Perhaps the clearest is that a business that shows less volatility can generally borrow money at lower interest rates, because lenders fear unpredictability. Another factor is that stock prices tend to decline when the company fails to meet its announced target, whether the actual performance is above or below the target.

Another type of revenue management, not mentioned in the case, is the *big bath*. If a company sees that it is going to come out below its target at the end of the current period, it uses this as an opportunity to write off bad debts, depreciate aging equipment, and so forth. This makes the results look even worse, but presumably the market treats a 20% shortfall as not much worse than a 10% shortfall. If the company is going to get wet, it may as well take a big bath and look better in the next period.

A good deal of revenue management is possible within the confines of GAAP, although Nortel's practices in this case appear to violate GAAP.

One might argue that revenue management can serve a legitimate purpose by providing a truer picture of the firm. The numbers may be abnormally low this quarter because the company is just about to make a big sale next quarter and abnormally high next quarter for the same reason. Smoothing avoids this problem and may avoid creating unwarranted alarm or euphoria. Given this, is it ethical?

The dilemma arises because we want a single number to sum up a more complicated situation. Ideally stakeholders and investors would look at the context rather than fixate on a single number. But the world is not ideal.

As for Nortel, its purpose in smoothing income is not to obtain a more accurate picture of the firm but to report performance that matches the projections. Is its conduct ethical?

### UTILITARIAN ANALYSIS

When income smoothing provides a truer picture of the firm, it may pass the utilitarian test. It gives a boost to the company at least in the short term and therefore benefits its owners and employees. The utilitarian test requires, of course, that everyone's utility be considered, not just the firm's. Yet income smoothing of this sort may result in more rational investment, which would benefit society at large. If so, it passes the utilitarian test.

However, there is a risk that the practice may be exposed, which could harm the company's reputation, particularly if it violates GAAP. This reduces utility in general because of the disruption and waste it creates—company initiatives are shut down, employees laid off, customers disappointed, investment capital squandered, and so forth. Managers must judge whether this risk is high enough that income smoothing results in a lower expected utility than literal reporting. The point here is not that income smoothing is ethical if the company can get away with it. The point is that the utilitarian calculation is affected by whether the company can get away with it. The other conditions for rational choice must be met as well.

One alternative is to report the literal numbers but explain the context as prominently as possible. This could result in the greatest overall utility, depending on the circumstances.

There is no indication in this case that Nortel's smoothing provides a truer picture of the firm. It is intended simply to bring revenue in line with the target. The utilitarian trade-off is therefore

more problematic in Nortel's case. Again, the smoothing may benefit the firm in the short run, but it distorts investment and carries a significant risk of reputation backlash.

A more basic analysis is also in order. The root idea of utilitarianism is that we should get straight on what our ultimate goals are and act to achieve them rather than something else. Anything else is irrational. Nortel managers do not appear to be rational from this point of view. They are acting as though their overriding goal is to meet certain numerical targets, no more and no less. But this is surely not their true goal. Ultimately they want to run a successful business, build a useful product, provide meaningful employment, or something of this sort. Achieving some degree of predictability in company performance may help achieve this goal, but it is only one factor among many. An *overriding* concern with numerical targets doesn't make sense.

### GENERALIZATION TEST

Nortel's income smoothing is a clear violation of the generalization test, because it is deceptive. Its purpose in smoothing revenue is to cause stakeholders to believe that revenue in a given period is something other than what it actually is, in order to benefit the firm in the short run. However, if firms always misstated revenue in this fashion whenever it would benefit them, no one would believe the numbers. People cannot be deceived if they don't believe the deception. So, generalizing the action defeats its purpose, which means that the action fails the generalization test.

It is slightly harder to analyze smoothing when it is designed to convey a truer picture of the firm's performance. One might argue that reporting literal numbers is as deceptive as reporting smoothed numbers. Reporting smoothed numbers is deceptive because it misleads stakeholders about what actually occurred in a given period. Reporting literal numbers is deceptive because it can give stakeholders an inaccurate understanding of the firm's overall performance, which is the main purpose of financial reporting, after all. What is one to do?

One must run the generalization test on both actions and see how it comes out. The easier case is reporting the literal numbers. It is deceptive in a way, but the purpose of the action does not depend on deception. The purpose is to convey what actually happened in a given period. If all companies reported the literal numbers, they would continue to convey what actually happened. Literal reporting may mislead stakeholders about the overall state of the firm, but they would continue to be misled if everyone reported the literal numbers. Even if they would no longer be misled, this would not defeat the purpose of the action, because misleading people is not part of its purpose.

However, reporting smoothed numbers for the purpose of providing a truer picture of the firm's performance may not be generalizable. Suppose firms always smoothed income when it would provide a truer picture. The problem is that there is no standard for how, and how much, firms will smooth their income for this purpose. Some firms may be very conservative, and others may abuse the privilege. As a result, the stakeholder doesn't really know what is going on in the firm. Generalizing the smoothing practice therefore defeats its purpose of giving people a truer picture of the firm.

If there were guidelines for how to smooth, that would be a different matter. In fact, one might argue that staying within GAAP provides enough limits on smoothing that the stakeholder can still infer meaningful information about the firm from the smoothed numbers. If so, then smoothing within GAAP is generalizable—but only if it is smoothing for the purpose of giving a truer picture of the firm, not for the purpose of meeting predefined targets.

## VIRTUE ETHICS

Nortel's income smoothing practices seriously compromise the virtue of its accountants, because it is inconsistent with who they are as professionals. An accountant is someone who makes a firm visible to managers and stakeholders. By instructing them to conceal what is happening in the firm, Nortel is asking its accountants not to be accountants. This is fundamentally inconsistent and intolerable. The only rational course for an accountant is to get out of this situation.

Income smoothing for the sake of providing a truer picture of the firm is a different matter. The accountant realizes that a single number, whether smoothed or not, cannot unambiguously convey the state of the firm. While struggling with this issue, the accountant may come down on one side or the other (ideally while passing the utilitarian and generalization tests). But so long as the accountant makes a good faith effort to convey the true state of the firm, there is no violation of virtue ethics.

## CONCLUSION

Nortel's income soothing practices probably violate the utilitarian test by failing to maximize utility, but they certainly violate it on a more fundamental level because Nortel's actions are not rationally aligned with its goals. The smoothing practices definitely violate the generalization test as well as virtue ethics. In a word, they are unethical.

Income smoothing for the purpose of providing a truer picture of the firm may pass the utilitarian test, but only under certain conditions, because there is a risk it can harm the firm as well as society at large. It fails the generalization test if the smoothing is inconsistent with GAAP. It passes the test if (a) it is consistent with GAAP, (b) GAAP standards are strict enough that stakeholders would be able to infer the true state of the firm if all firms were to use smoothing within GAAP. Smoothing to provide a truer picture of the firm is consistent with virtue ethics if the accountant makes a good faith effort to provide the least misleading numbers. ▪

---

## CASE 6.2

# Tires and Rollovers

### SYNOPSIS[2]

Firestone Tire and Rubber Company, founded by Harvey Firestone in 1900, was a pioneer in the mass production of tires and the original supplier to Ford Motor Company. Despite its distinguished history, the company lost its competitive edge in the 1970s and eventually sold out to the Japanese firm Bridgestone in 1988.

Bridgestone Firestone continued to encounter quality problems, however. The trouble began when Ford Explorer SUVs started having rollover accidents in the 1990s due to tread separation in their Firestone tires. It was at first unclear whether the problems were due to improper inflation, hot weather, defects in the tires, or design problems with Ford's SUVs. Now we know that all four factors played a role. Although tire pressure and heat exacerbated the situation, Firestone tires clearly had quality problems, particularly tires manufactured during a labor dispute at the Firestone plant in Decatur, Illinois.

One issue in the dispute was Bridgestone Firestone's proposal to switch to 12-hour shifts. Line managers warned of a decline in quality, because it is well established that long hours compromise both quality and efficiency. Despite a strike at the plant, Bridgestone Firestone eventually won the dispute and installed the long shifts.

Ford wasn't innocent, either, because its SUVs had been rolling over since the 1980s, due in part to a high center of gravity. Bridgestone Firestone recalled 6.5 million tires in 2000 and closed the Decatur plant in 2001. Ford redesigned the Explorer in 2001.

### THE ISSUES

This well-publicized case raises at least three ethical issues. One is the direct and obvious issue of what to do when your company's tires are defective. A second concerns the labor relations practices that apparently underlay many of the quality problems at Bridgestone Firestone. A third is how to deal with the cross-cultural dynamic that arose when Japanese managers and board members were involved in running a subsidiary in the United States.

This particular case study does not tell the cross-cultural story, and so we will not address it here. Nonetheless, it is an interesting story, in part because Bridgestone Firestone's Japanese executives had a history of behaving as inappropriately in Japan, as measured by Japanese norms, as they did in the United States, as measured by American norms.

## PRODUCT RECALL—UTILITARIAN TEST

To focus the safety issue, let's deal specifically with the tire recall. When is there an ethical obligation to recall an unsafe product?

The utilitarian test balances the cost of a recall against the risk of injuries. Risk is notoriously hard to assess, and there is no really satisfactory way to do it. For product safety issues, one simple and reasonable approach is to compute the expected number of injuries, assume that this many people will actually be injured, and try to measure the disutility that results. If one tire in 100,000 causes a rollover (just to pick a number), and 6.5 million tires are subject to recall, we can assume that 65 accidents will result if the tires are not recalled, perhaps spanning the range from minor to more serious. To weigh this against the cost of a recall, we can ask: How much would we be willing to pay to avoid each type of injury to ourselves? Or we could estimate all the medical and other expenses incurred by such an injury, and add in a penalty for pain and suffering that might be assessed in a typical lawsuit. If the cost of the recall is greater than the total cost of the 65 injuries, then failure to recall passes the utilitarian test.

This approach may seem suspect, because it brings to mind the infamous Ford Pinto affair of the 1960s. Ford refused to fix the gasoline tank because this would cost the company more than the lawsuits that would result from exploding tanks. This decision resulted in criminal prosecution of some Ford executives for manslaughter, although they were acquitted due to lack of evidence. There is no suggestion here, however, that we should treat tires as Ford treated the Pinto. We are considering the costs to everyone, not just to the company. Furthermore, the utilitarian test is only *one* of the tests we are applying. Even if a failure to recall passes the utilitarian test, it may be unethical on other grounds. Nonetheless, the utilitarian test is important, since it is irrational to spend a king's fortune to reduce a minuscule risk to zero. At some point, we must weigh the risk against the cost of avoiding it.

## GENERALIZATION TEST

Selling someone a product implies a promise. If a restaurant serves me a pizza, the cook promises me that it is safe to eat. This promise is reflected in the legal doctrine of implied warranty: Any product sold carries the guarantee that it is fit for the purpose for which it is sold.

It is unethical to break this promise because breaking promises in general, merely to benefit oneself, fails the generalization test. Breaking an implied warranty in particular is ungeneralizable, because the only reason you can sell someone a defective product is that merchants normally sell products that do what they are supposed to do. Otherwise the customer would check out the product carefully and refuse to buy it.

You can promise something only if it is under your control. The pizza chef can promise me a safe pizza because the ingredients are under his control. He knows what is in the pizza because he made it. In manufacturing, some factors can be controlled and some cannot. This is addressed by designing the production process so that the uncontrollable factors are random, and the defects occur according to a known distribution. Statistical sampling can then estimate the probability of a random defect. The same sampling procedure can detect whether the defects become nonrandom, which indicates a malfunction in the controllable part of the process. Thus quality can be assured by controlling what one can control, verifying that the remaining variations are random, and reducing the probability of a random defect almost to zero. This is the principle behind quality control techniques, which allow manufacturers to keep their promise to deliver a safe product.

Bridgestone Firestone therefore has a duty is to remove all causes of defects over which it has control. To this day, no one can put a finger on a specific defect in the tires that Firestone could control. Yet their failure rates were much higher than the industry average, perhaps due to Firestone's handling of labor relations. We will argue below that Firestone could have improved quality through good management, which means it had some degree of control over the risk. It must therefore recall the tires to keep its promise to customers.

The argument is not that Firestone broke a promise simply because it had a poorer safety record than its competitors. The fact that other brands were safer is relevant only because it suggests that Firestone had enough *control* to make its tires safer. If nothing else, it could have mimicked the quality procedures and labor management practices of its competitors.

One might propose a separate and additional argument that Bridgestone Firestone made an implied promise to sell a product as safe as competing products, or at least as safe as products with a similar price. In general, this sort of argument is problematic. The mere act of selling a product does not imply that it is as safe as competing products. No one expects a Ferrari to be as safe as a Hummer, even if the price is the same. If a Ferrari were sold as an automobile that is as safe as any, and if this were part of the marketing, then that would be another matter. In Bridgestone Firestone's case, one might argue that a tire is nothing if it is not a safe tire, and marketing a tire sends an implied message that it is as safe as other tires. Even if this argument fails, however, one can argue as above that the company broke its implied warranty, which does not depend on what other manufacturers were doing.

## LABOR RELATIONS

The generalizability argument above relies on the assumption that the defects were largely due to bad management practices over which Firestone had control. Let's have a look at these practices.

As already noted, some managers on the plant floor feared that a switch to 12-hour shifts would compromise quality. Although some labor leaders claimed that scabs were responsible for the defective tires, a study of the Decatur plant by two Princeton economists found that most of the bad tires were manufactured before the strike began and when the unionized workers joined replacement workers after the strike.[3] The study concluded that poor labor relations, more than untrained replacement workers, resulted in substandard tires.[4]

Firestone was known as a well-managed company prior to the 1970s but stumbled badly when Michelin introduced radial tires in 1972. John Nevin took over as CEO to turn Firestone around after the company's first huge recall in the late 1970s. It was an era when downsizing and restructuring were the rage—and Japanese companies were rising stars. Nevin ordered massive layoffs and broke long-standing relationships with employees, suppliers, and customers. He was initially successful, but the company succumbed to the wave of Japanese takeovers in the industry when it sold out to Bridgestone.

Twelve-hour shifts became trendy with executives in the 1990s, and Firestone jumped on this bandwagon as well. The union charged that Bridgestone Firestone's investment in U.S. plants was inadequate, another legacy of the 1980s. Management denied this, but the Decatur plant was clearly behind the times. Tires were manufactured largely by hand, and quality control was substandard.

The net result was a disgruntled workforce, particularly in the five U.S. plants that were struck in the mid-1990s. Employees got the message that the company was more concerned about the latest cost-cutting fads than product quality. All of this was within management control.

## VIRTUE ETHICS

There is another issue at stake. Virtue ethics argues that our actions should be consistent with who we are. Yet Bridgestone Firestone put its Decatur employees in a position that was fundamentally inconsistent. The company asked them to be tire manufacturers, which means that they worked in an industry that is all about safety. A tire is a tire is a tire, but it must be a safe tire. At the same time, the company would not allow the employees to be serious about safe tires. It made them work long shifts that compromised quality, it hired unqualified replacement workers, and it denied them technology and quality control practices available in other plants. In a word, the company was asking employees to make safe tires and not to make safe tires. This is not only bad in a utilitarian sense, because it ads to sour attitudes and unsafe tires, but it is fundamentally inconsistent and unethical on that ground alone.

## CONCLUSION

Bridgestone Firestone's conduct was ungeneralizable because it violated an implied warranty, and it was contrary to virtue ethics. Further study is required to determine whether it complied with the utilitarian principle.

The company should have applied all measures under its control to ensure the safety of its product, including the upgrading of its Decatur plant and adoption of management practices known to be conducive to quality. ▪

## CASE 6.3

# The Bullard Houses

## SYNOPSIS[5]

The Bullard Houses are a group of connected townhouses next to the downtown financial district. They were once residences for the rich and fashionable but fell into dereliction. Now that the inner city has begun to gentrify again, the property is an attractive location for development. Surviving members of the Bullard family own the property and want it to be developed in a way that preserves the houses and avoids what they see as distasteful commercial use. They would particularly like to see them renovated as luxury condominiums.

Four firms are bidding for the property with various plans for its redevelopment. The firm most relevant here is Absentia, Ltd., a Bahamian blind trust. It is working through a local and re-spected real estate firm, Jones & Jones, but it secretly repre-sents the Conrad Milton Hotel Group. Milton wants to build a high-rise hotel on the garden next to the houses and convert the historical building into a lobby and meeting rooms. The Absentia representatives have explicit instructions not to reveal these plans during negotiation.

Is it ethical for the Absentia representatives to conceal the true intention behind their bid?

## GOOD FAITH NEGOTIATION

To determine what sort of information should be conveyed during negotiation, we must recall the purpose of negotiation. The purpose is to arrive at a mutually beneficial agreement. I am willing to sell you a car when the car is worth less to me than the money I get from you. Conversely, the money must be worth less to you than the car.

Negotiation therefore presupposes that we can both assess the value of the items we will receive in the exchange. I don't have to tell you everything about the car. It is enough to tell you where the car is and give you an opportunity to check it out. On the other hand, I shouldn't *deceive* you about the car, because deception is ungeneralizable. I shouldn't tell you that the car gets 30 miles per gallon when it does not.

Good faith negotiation therefore requires the following:

- *Principle 1. Each party should (a) tell the other exactly what will be conveyed, (b) provide enough information about the items conveyed to allow the other to assess their worth, and (c) avoid deceiving the other party.*

Anything less is ungeneralizable and unethical.

## WHAT CAN BE CONCEALED

Interestingly, there is no obligation for me to tell you *what the car is worth to me.* Perhaps I can't drive, and I would be willing to sell the car at any price to get rid of it. But I have no obligation to say anything about this. The reason is that negotiation is still possible when, as a general practice, neither party reveals anything about what the deal is worth to himself or herself. In fact, negotiation is possible *only* when both parties are reticent about this.

Think about it this way. I have a minimum price at which I will sell, and you have a maximum price at which you will buy. If my minimum is less than or equal to your maximum, a deal is possible. But negotiation must somehow arrive at a particular price. If I reveal my minimum and you your maximum, I will insist on the minimum price and you will insist on the maximum—and there is no deal. So I will offer a price above my minimum, which reveals limited information about what my minimum actually is. You will bid a lower price that is below your maximum, which reveals limited information about your maximum. Perhaps the process continues until the offers meet in the middle. Negotiation is therefore an exchange of signals that reveal just enough information to reach mutually agreeable terms.

Exactly how this proceeds varies widely depending on the context, but then it always requires concealing a certain amount of information about what is acceptable to the parties. The possibility of negotiation in general presupposes that the parties adhere to the prevailing signaling practices. We conclude:

- *Principle 2. Negotiation is ethical only if the parties conceal information about what is acceptable to them—the amount and nature of concealment depending on the context in which the negotiation takes place.*

## GENERALIZATION TEST

Milton's plans to build a hotel affect the price it is willing to offer, but this fact imposes no obligation on Absentia to say anything about the intended use. In fact, Principle 2 implies that Absentia has an obligation to say as little as possible about it, consistent with the possibility of making a deal.

On the other hand, if the sales contract will promise that Milton won't build a hotel (or similar commercial enterprise), then Principle 1 says that Milton must be straightforward about its plans. Anything else would misinform the Bullards about the terms of the agreement.

The case description is unclear about whether a sales contract between Absentia and the Bullards would actually specify the use of the property. Perhaps the contract is not explicit on this point, but the Bullards are willing to sell because they believe that the property will not be developed commercially. There are at least two scenarios: (a) The Bullards ask how the property will be developed, and Absentia lies—it says development plans are noncommercial, undecided, unknown, or whatever. (b) The Bullards don't ask, but Absentia knows that they are willing to close the deal because they falsely believe the development will probably be noncommercial.

Scenario (a) involves an out-and-out lie. Lying, simply to benefit oneself, is normally unethical because it is deceptive, and deception is ungeneralizable.

One might argue that there is a special rationale for deception in this case, a rationale that may be generalizable—namely, Principle 2 requires it. However, Principle 2 requires only that Absentia reveal as little as possible about what deal it would find acceptable. It is possible to do this without deception. Consider the car sale. If you ask me what my lowest price is, I can answer vaguely or dodge the question. I can even repeat my current offer and say "this is my best offer" without necessarily deceiving you. Deception is causing you to believe something that I know is false. Such remarks don't deceive because no one takes them seriously in negotiation. They are part of the signaling game. Everyone knows that negotiation can't work if such information is fully revealed. Similarly, Absentia can state that it has not been authorized to discuss plans for the property. This is literally true, and it is not deceptive—unless it *causes* the Bullards to believe that the development will be noncommercial, which seems unlikely.

Absentia might respond that if the car dealer can say "this is my best offer" without deception, because such remarks are part of the game, then Absentia should be able to say, "We have no plans for commercial development." But the remarks are not parallel. "This is my best offer" creates no deception because it speaks only to the terms that the dealer is willing to accept. It has no further implications that are relevant to whether the other party will make a deal. However, "we have no plans for commercial development" does more than speak to the terms Absentia is willing to accept. It has implications for whether the Bullards will make a deal.

Because Principle 2 does not require lying, there is no apparent rationale for Absentia to lie in this case, other than the fact that it benefits Absentia. The lie is therefore ungeneralizable and unethical.

Scenario (b) is trickier to analyze. Because the Bullards already believe that Absentia probably won't develop the site commercially, Absentia might argue that what it says or doesn't say cannot *cause* them to believe this. So it can keep quiet without deceiving them.

However, Absentia's silence may deceive the Bullards about the *evidence base* for their beliefs. To take an analogy, suppose Joe has an abdominal pain but believes it is nothing serious. The doctor performs a battery of tests and shows all but one test result to Joe. He says nothing about the one test that indicates cancer. In this case, silence is deception, because Joe expects the doctor to show him any relevant test results, and the doctor knows that Joe expects this. The doctor doesn't cause Joe to believe falsely that his illness is minor, because Joe already believes this. But it causes him to believe falsely that there is no evidence of a serious illness.

Thus, we can ask whether the Bullards would expect Absentia to reveal any commercial development plans, and if so, whether Absentia knows that they expect it. The case description doesn't make this clear, but there is no reason a priori to suppose that the Bullards would expect Absentia to reveal plans it is not asked about. The Bullards presumably base their judgment on their knowledge of the situation, the reputation of Jones & Jones, and so forth. So it is hard to say that Absentia's silence *causes* the Bullards to have false beliefs about the evidence base for their expectations. Its silence therefore passes the generalization test.

## VIRTUE ETHICS

Negotiation takes place not only between companies but also between human beings who represent the companies. We concluded that Absentia can ethically fail to correct the Bullards' expectations about development of their property. This is because the Bullards would not expect a *company* to volunteer such information.

When human beings sit down to talk, however, the equation changes. If the Bullards could sell the property by going to the Absentia Web site and clicking the right boxes, then human relationships would not enter the picture. But a deal of this magnitude requires that human beings work it out. The possibility of human engagement, even communication, presupposes a certain amount of honesty and candor. It presupposes not only that people avoid deceiving each other, but that they in some sense *level* with each other. As we say in Western cultures, they must be willing to look each other in the eye. Relating authentically with others is part of being human, and therefore a virtue.

When Absentia representatives sit down with negotiators for the Bullards, it is hard to imagine how they could look them in the eye, knowing their concern about the future of their property, without saying what they know about the hotel plans. Or to put it differently, the Bullards may not expect a company to volunteer information, but their representatives might very well expect fellow human beings to relate to them authentically.[6]

One might argue that Western-style business makes a distinction between business relationships and personal relationships. It is true that other, relationship-based business cultures may not make this distinction, and in them it is important to relate to all business associates on a personal level. (Interestingly, direct eye contact is normally inappropriate in these cultures.) But this is not necessary in Western business culture. One can in fact make a case that the Western style of business relationship pressures people to neglect such virtues as loyalty, friendship, and authenticity. Yet virtue requires that we resist this pressure.

The basic rule of virtue ethics is that it is inconsistent and therefore unethical to compromise a virtue, except for the sake of another virtue. There is no general competing virtue at stake for the Absentia negotiator. There is a fiduciary duty to advance the interests of the Conrad Milton Company, but this is not required by loyalty in the Aristotelian sense—which is owed to human beings, not to business firms. There may be competing loyalties at stake for particular negotiators, for instance, if they cannot support their families unless this particular deal goes through. In such cases, inauthenticity may pass the virtue test, although it must meet the other conditions for rational choice as well.

One might question whether negotiation itself compromises authenticity, because we have argued that it requires a certain amount of concealment. It is interesting to note that some relationship-based cultures try to avoid Western-style negotiation between business partners, because it disrupts personal relationships or group harmony. Yet negotiation need not compromise virtue if the parties withhold information only to the extent necessary to make negotiation possible, and if both understand that this is going on and why.

## CONCLUSION

It is ethical for Absentia to withhold information about its development plans from the Bullards, if the sole effect is to conceal the price and other terms to which Absentia would be willing to agree. It is unethical, however, to tell the Bullards that there are no plans for commercial development of their property, whether or not this becomes part of the contract.

If the Bullards agree to sell on the basis of their mistaken belief that Absentia will not develop it commercially, then Absentia can fail to correct their belief without violating generalizability. Yet individual Absentia negotiators should mention the development plans to their counterparts to avoid compromising personal virtue, unless this obligation is overridden by conflicting loyalties.

This is not meant to imply that there are different standards for personal morality and professional morality. There is one morality, and all moral actions must meet the three conditions of rational choice. In the present case, the action in question may fail the virtue test while passing the others. ■

## CASE 6.4

# Marketing Prozac and Paxil

## SYNOPSIS[7]

The antidepressant drugs Prozac and Paxil are "selective serotonin reuptake inhibitors." Low levels of the neurotransmitter serotonin are associated with depression and other psychological disorders. The drugs slow the rate at which serotonin is reabsorbed, which means that it is present longer and in greater quantity. Partly due to direct-to-consumer marketing by the pharmaceutical firm Lilly, Prozac became widely used not only as an antidepressant but also as a means to "improve" one's personality. GlaxoSmithKline's Paxil took on a similar role when the U.S. FDA approved it as a treatment for social anxiety disorder. Some Paxil advertisements contained a questionnaire that consumers could use to "determine" whether they have such a disorder.

## ISSUES

The case raises several ethical issues, including the following:

- Is direct-to-consumer marketing of prescription drugs ethical? It is much less regulated in the United States than in some other countries.
- Is it ethical to encourage consumers to use a drug that makes them more socially acceptable? People sometimes use Prozac or Paxil to make them less shy or more extroverted.
- Is it ethical for marketing campaigns to encourage self-diagnosis?

## DIRECT-TO-CONSUMER MARKETING

Direct-to-consumer marketing of prescription drugs is a "pull" strategy that encourages consumers to ask their physicians for the drugs. One can ask whether physicians should be influenced by patients' requests for a drug, but that is another issue. The issue is whether a pharmaceutical company should encourage people to go to the doctor's office and ask for it.

It may be helpful to look at an analogous case. Suppose the news media widely report the benefits of Prozac, and as a result many people become aware of it and ask their physicians for it. This seems rather innocent, since the media are only providing information. Yet an advertising campaign that creates a desire for Prozac may seem suspect.

Reasoning by analogy cannot resolve an ethical issue. At some point, one must apply the criteria for rational choice. But an analogy can be "therapeutic" by helping us to think more clearly.

Let's first think about media coverage of Prozac. It seems all right, unless it leads to such widespread abuse of Prozac that public knowledge causes more harm than good. It is similar to reporting the

explosive properties of fertilizer, which seems perfectly innocent unless it causes terrorists to make bombs. In other words, dissemination of information seems all right unless it fails a utilitarian test.

However, an advertising campaign for Prozac may seem suspect even if it passes the utilitarian test. It may psychologically "manipulate" consumers to want something they wouldn't otherwise desire. This kind of advertising may seem wrong—even if it causes as much benefit as nonmanipulative advertising.

So we distinguish two issues: Does public awareness of Prozac pass the utilitarian test? Even if it does, can Prozac advertising still be wrong, perhaps because it "manipulates" consumers by creating desire?

First, the utilitarian issue. The publicity surrounding Prozac was enormous, due in part to the book *Listening to Prozac* and general "buzz" in the media. This led to abuse of the drug, but it also brought relief to many people who were clinically depressed and would otherwise have gone untreated. So Prozac ads may well have maximized utility. Until someone presents evidence to the contrary, there is no clear utilitarian case against direct-to-consumer marketing of Prozac.[8]

If the ads are to maximize utility, however, they must be designed to minimize abuse by honestly reporting the limitations and side effects of the drug—and above all, the complications of withdrawal. Prozac requires months to take effect, can have serious side effects, is no more effective than its predecessors, and creates a dependency that causes problems if one stops taking it. Too many warnings could of course deter legitimate users, but an ethical ad must present a balanced picture that maximizes overall utility. The same applies to media coverage.

## CREATING DESIRE

Now let's examine whether it is ethical to create desire for Prozac. No one questions that it is OK to create desire among clinically depressed individuals. They don't desire Prozac until they know it exists, and they learn from advertising that it exists. Advertising creates a desire for Prozac in this sense, and this is perfectly ethical.

The ethical problem lies in creating a desire *for the benefits of Prozac* as well as for Prozac itself. Clinically depressed people already desire the benefits of Prozac. But advertising convinces people who are not clinically depressed that they shouldn't be so shy, that they should be more extroverted, that they should be the life of the party, and that Prozac can fix them. The advertising does more than provide information. In popular parlance, it works "subconsciously."

This is obviously a general issue with advertising, which people often describe as operating at a "subconscious" level. This is deeply problematic in Western ethics because it fails to respect individual autonomy. It is not so much that psychological manipulation is ungeneralizable; it is irrational in a deeper sense. In the

Western tradition, a moral agent is someone who acts on the basis of a consciously formulated rationale. Psychological manipulation, if it means anything, refers to an attempt to subvert this kind of decision making. It therefore takes away someone's agency. It is basically murder—albeit temporary murder, because agency can normally be recovered as soon as the manipulation stops.

There is also an element of deception in psychological manipulation.[9] If ads were not deceptive, then advertisers would be willing to warn consumers that ads are manipulative. But they are not willing to do so. Deception is normally wrong because it is ungeneralizable.

One can argue that "advertising speech" can lie without deceiving and is therefore ethical. An ad that calls its product "the best buy on the market," when it is not, doesn't deceive anyone because people expect hyperbole from ads. OK, if people expect Prozac ads to be hyperbolic and as a result are neither deceived nor manipulated, then the ads are ethical.

One can create desire without manipulation. A doctor can create a strong desire for cancer treatment, for example, by showing a patient some test results. This is not manipulation because the desire is the psychological result of rational persuasion. So a Prozac ad that makes a rational, above-board, and honest case for extroverted behavior—it is good for your career, or whatever—can create desire without violating autonomy. However, an ad that appeals subconsciously to insecurities or longings is unethical.

This sounds rather stern, since it appears to rule out appealing to emotions for any purpose. Is it wrong for an ad to appeal to sympathy to solicit contributions for starving children? If sympathy means an emotional reaction, yes. An emotional reaction may be the inevitable result of rational persuasion, but this is another matter. It is OK to describe what it is like to be hungry and to portray poverty in graphic detail, even though this portrayal may cause emotional distress, because this kind of information is relevant to making a rational choice. But the appeal should ultimately be to the rational mind.

There are cases in which autonomy can be overridden for a greater cause, as when someone may use an emotional appeal to get hostages released. One might argue in such cases that the hostage taker had already sacrificed autonomy, since, in Western ethics, one is an agent only to the extent that one acts ethically. None of this discussion, incidentally, is meant to imply that it is wrong for Shakespeare to work on the emotions of his audience. His intent is not to induce action but to deepen our understanding of ourselves.

So far, we have found no reason to conclude that direct-to-consumer marketing of Prozac is in itself unethical. Manipulative Prozac ads, however, are unethical—not because they create a desire for Prozac, but because they are manipulative.

## BEING SOCIALLY ACCEPTABLE

One may view Prozac ads as objectionable even when they do not manipulate, because they are deceptive in another way. Even if they make a perfectly rational case for extroverted behavior, they imply that consumers need this kind of behavior to achieve their goals, when they do not. They are like ads for breast enlargement or hair transplant. They perpetuate the myth that people cannot obtain satisfaction without socially admired physical traits.

Ads for Prozac and other self-enhancing products are clearly unethical if they perpetuate what the advertisers know to be a myth, because this is a form of deception. However, an ad that makes an honest and unexaggerated case for the benefits of a product does not have this problem. While big breasts or hair may not change anyone's life, a less-shy personality could have career advantages for some people.

Yet some would object to Prozac ads even when they make an honest case for its benefits. They believe people should be less concerned about social acceptability. If they are shy, they should accept themselves as they are, other people should accept them, and so forth.

This appears to be a utilitarian argument, because it suggests that marketing Prozac supports social norms that make us less happy or satisfied. The utilitarian test, however, is not whether we would be better off in a different kind of society. The test is whether we would be better off without direct-to-consumer marketing of Prozac in particular. One would have to make a case that Lilly can single-handedly affect social norms. Given the sensation that Prozac created, this idea is not completely implausible. But to establish a utilitarian obligation, one would have to make a stronger case than we have now.

## TEMPTATION

Another potential problem with Prozac ads is that even when they are honest and nonmanipulative, they nonetheless tempt people to take a drug that is not good for them.

Many people who are not clinically depressed want to feel better about themselves. They know that feeling better is not worth the risk of taking a psychoactive drug that creates dependence. Yet they are tempted by the Prozac ads—not because the ads play on their emotions, but because the ads simply lay out the facts. It is like a waiter in a restaurant who tells you about the delicious chocolate cake you can order for dessert. The waiter is simply stating the facts; the cake is delicious. Nonetheless, the suggestion may tempt you to eat something you rationally decided you should avoid.

Temptation is a major issue in marketing. Restaurants constantly push high-calorie hamburgers, French fries, and desserts. They cover the table with photos of these sinful indulgences to make sure the temptation is constant. We can't even go through the checkout line at a bookstore without resisting the chocolate candy displays at the register.

Snack foods are loaded with salt and sugar to make sure we can't eat just one. Then there are products that create a physiological dependence, such as cigarettes, alcohol, and recreational drugs. One the user is hooked, they create a temptation that is particularly hard to resist.

Temptation can be manipulative and deceptive, but it need not be. It may simply make us aware of a product that happens to be very tempting. It does not deny autonomy, but only makes us work harder to maintain autonomy. The waiter's recommendation makes it harder to stick to my decision to avoid dessert, but it doesn't prevent me from sticking to it. So temptation must be analyzed differently than manipulative or deceptive advertising.

The argument against temptation seems to be utilitarian. If temptation works, people may do things that are bad for them. If it doesn't work, people must nonetheless struggle to resist temptation, which makes life less pleasant. Either way we lose. On the other hand, it is perfectly OK to tempt people to eat celery (provided the temptation is not manipulative) because it passes a utilitarian test. If only we could find ad wizards who could tempt us in this way. Temptation becomes wrong only when it reduces utility.

The usual response to this argument is that marketers don't force people to eat French fries or take Prozac, but only give them the choice. (Marketing to children is another matter.) There is no obligation to protect people from themselves. The problem with this response is that it begs the question. The issue is precisely whether there is an obligation to protect people from themselves. Simply to state a position without argument gets us nowhere. Actually we have an argument, a utilitarian argument, that temptation can be unethical. As far as Prozac is concerned, we concluded above that there is no clear utilitarian argument against marketing Prozac directly to consumers, due to the benefits for clinically depressed individuals. So tempting people with Prozac passes the utilitarian test. The outcome could be different with other products, however.

## SELF-DIAGNOSIS

Once it received approval to market Paxil as a treatment for social anxiety disorder, GlaxoSmithKline publicized a self-test for the disorder. Consumers answer questions about their behavior and are told that if they receive a certain score on the test, they may have social anxiety disorder and should ask their doctor about Paxil.

People with social anxiety disorder have a strong fear of embarrassment or being judged in social situations. Their fear can result in debilitating symptoms, such as panic attacks, and it can substantially restrict their activities and success in life. A self-test can identify people with this disorder, people who would otherwise not go to a doctor because they are unaware that effective treatment exists.

GlaxoSmithKline has been accused of building a self-test that too readily identifies people as having social anxiety disorder. To be ethical, a self-test must obviously avoid deception and an excessive number of false positives. But it is hard to see why encouraging self-diagnosis is necessarily deceptive or otherwise ungeneralizable, or why it would necessarily fail a utilitarian test. People must self-diagnose to some extent whenever they call the doctor. They decide whether they have a routine virus that will pass in a few days, or something more serious that requires medical attention. Some guidance in this area only improves a process that already occurs. In fact, one might make a utilitarian case that there should be more information on self-diagnosis, as well as professional standards for such information.

On the other hand, the practice of giving a *test* is somewhat suspect. Why not just tell the consumer, "If you have symptoms X, Y, Z, then you ought to see your doctor about possible social anxiety disorder." Probably because there is something magical about a test score. It carries authority, much as a physician's diagnosis. One might say that a test score is common sense in a white coat. So the test is basically smoke and mirrors. It is deceptive because it gives a false impression of authority.

## CONCLUSION

Direct-to-consumer marketing of Prozac is ethical if it is nonmanipulative in the sense explained above and if it balances the benefits with possible side effects and withdrawal difficulties. Marketing of Paxil can ethically include honest advice for when one ought to see a physician about possible social anxiety disorder. However, a self-test that generates a score is a bit of humbug and should be avoided. ■

---

## CASE 6.5

# Countrywide Financial and Subprime Mortgages

### SYNOPSIS[10]

In 2007, Countrywide Financial was the largest mortgage lender in the United States. About 9% of its loans were subprime, meaning that the borrower paid higher interest rates and fees due to a bad credit history. Many of the subprime loans were going bad because of falling house prices, and the company found itself at the center of the U.S. subprime mortgage crisis.

Within 18 months, the mortgage crisis metastasized into a global financial crisis. Credit markets froze in the last half of 2008, due to the repackaging of subprime loans into "poison" mortgage-backed securities. Outstanding credit default swaps amounting to $62 trillion, often backed by inadequate capital reserves, magnified the problem. Stock values fell precipitously worldwide. Foreclosure rates and bank failures rose sharply. Massive government bailouts and related actions were undertaken. The U.S., EU, and Japanese economies quickly went into recession.

As for Countrywide, its CEO, Angelo Mozilo, initially spoke of an "over-reaction" to the subprime lending crisis and to his company's role.[11] He noted that some 20–25% of U.S. mortgage loans were subprime at the time, compared to less than 10% at Countrywide. Yet the company began an unstoppable slide and finally sold out to Bank of America in July 2008 for one-sixth of its value a year earlier.

Many critics questioned the ethics of subprime lending at Countrywide and elsewhere. A common practice was to offer "2/28" loans that have a low, fixed interest rate for the first two years but much higher, floating interest rates for the remaining 28 years of the loan. Borrowers were told that they could refinance after two years to reduce monthly payments. This might have worked if house prices kept rising, but they fell. Many loans were soon "under water," meaning that borrower owed more than the house was worth. Thousands of borrowers were unable to refinance and were stuck with payments that were sometimes twice as high as before. If they could not the make the payments, lenders generally foreclose, in many cases taking a loss.

## THE ISSUES

Two main issues arise with respect to subprime mortgages. Should Countrywide and other lenders have sold subprime mortgages, at least in the way they did, or was this an unethical form of predatory lending? Should banks have foreclosed when borrowers could neither refinance nor meet ballooning payments, or should they have renegotiated the loans on terms more favorable to the borrower?

Defenders of subprime mortgages say that they give would-be homeowners a chance to redeem themselves and recover from past mistakes by establishing a new credit record. Critics say that the loans are predatory because customers are misled about the risks or are tempted into borrowing money they cannot repay.

The foreclosure issue is equally confusing. Some point out that borrowers are adults and should not take money they cannot repay. If we give them a break, it will only encourage borrowers to be irresponsible in the future. Others say that lenders should make accommodation to borrowers they exploited and misled for the sake of collecting high fees and interest rates.

We will try to shed some light on these issues by applying the principles of rational choice. The analysis isn't particularly short or simple, but why should we expect ethics to be easier than other fields?

The financial crisis exposed a number of ethically questionable practices in addition to subprime lending. Mortgage companies sold loans as soon as they made them, relieving themselves of any responsibility to collect payments and therefore of a clear incentive to award the loans responsibly. Financial institutions repackaged the loans onto mortgage-backed securities and sold them worldwide, in some cases leveraging themselves beyond all precedent in order to cash in on this lucrative market. Rating agencies gave the highest ratings to these securities, despite the obvious risk they entailed. Banks and insurance companies sold trillions of dollars worth of credit default swaps on mortgage-backed securities without adequate capital reserves, a practice that lulled even conservative Swiss banks into buying the securities. As the crisis deepened, some financial institutions whose risky investments led them to the brink of collapse accepted massive taxpayer-funded bailouts. After receiving these bailouts, they acquired a new reluctance to lend money to businesses, despite the need for economic stimulus, their own record profits, and their willingness to lend to almost anyone a year earlier. All of these issues deserve attention but go beyond the scope of the current analysis.

## SUBPRIME LENDING: UTILITARIAN TEST

We can begin by asking whether Countrywide's subprime loans resulted in greater expected utility than not making them.

The most directly affected are borrowers and company stockholders. If subprime loans were risky enough to result in an *expected* loss for the borrowers (i.e., the net expected value was negative), then the loans probably failed the utilitarian test and should not have been granted—even if they maximized expected revenue for the company. A loss for borrowers more than offsets an equal gain for stockholders, due to concave utility curves.

Things get more interesting if the expected value for borrowers was positive. This *could* have been the situation for Countrywide. Everyone seemed to think that house prices would continue to rise. After all, they had not fallen significantly in the United States since 1920. The relevant issue for the utilitarian test is not whether a rise in house prices was *in fact* probable, but whether it was *rational to believe* a rise was probable. As it happened, the market went sour, the company failed, and everybody lost. But this doesn't show that such an outcome was likely, much less that people were irrational in believing it was unlikely.

In any case, subprime loans in principle passed the utilitarian test if people were rational in believing that prices would, with high probability, continue to rise.

The design of the loans is another matter, however. The 2/28 scheme was quite draconian from the borrower's point of view. Terms that are kinder to the borrower, while still being financially viable, would have resulted in greater overall utility. Anyone with common sense knows this. So there was an ethical obligation to structure a different kind of loan.

One can ask whether it is consistent with the *other* ethical tests to make a loan with substantial risk, even when the expected return is positive. We will deal with this next.

## SUBPRIME LENDING: GENERALIZATION TEST

Even if we grant that subprime loans had positive expected value for customers, there was a great deal of risk. We can ask whether

Countrywide should have made sure customers understood the risk, and even if they understood it, whether the company should have tempted customers with risky loans. The company's actions may have failed the generalization test.

We don't know exactly how Countrywide dealt with its customers, but let's analyze the issue by applying the generalization test to some possible scenarios.

- *Scenario 1. The lender told the customer that the payments would double after two years, but said, "You can always refinance to reduce the payments."*

This was an outright lie, because the customer could not "always" refinance. Refinancing would be impossible if prices fell, or even if they didn't rise enough. Lying to a customer to make a sale fails the generalization test, because if salespeople always did this, customers would not believe them, and the lies would not achieve their purpose.

- *Scenario 2. The lender told the customer about the ballooning payments but said that "borrowers with this type of loan are refinancing after two years." The statement, we will suppose, was true at the time. But the customer inferred (incorrectly) from this remark that the option to refinance was a sure thing in the future. The lender knew that the customer misunderstood the risk but said nothing to correct the misunderstanding.*

In this case, there was no outright lie, but there was deception. To deceive is to cause someone to believe something you know is false. The lender's remark about refinancing was the cause of the false belief. Deception is ungeneralizable because if salespeople always caused people to have false beliefs to make a sale, customers would not be deceived. They would be on guard, ask questions, do some independent research, and so forth.

One might claim that the customer should have been on guard and done some research in any case, but this is only a claim, not an argument. Even if we establish that the customer "should" have done these things, this is not the same as showing that it is ethical for the lender to deceive him. The fact remains that deception fails the generalization test.

- *Scenario 3. The lender warned about larger payments in the future but, this time, said nothing about refinancing. However, there was reason for the lender to believe that the customer planned to refinance and was unaware of the risk—perhaps because the customer talked about it, or because*

*customers generally assumed that if a lender were willing to grant a loan, the risk must be manageable.*

- *Scenario 4. This is the same as the previous scenario, except that the lender had no particular reason to suspect that the customer was unaware of the risk.*
- *Scenario 5. The lender gave explicit warnings about all the risks, whether or not there was reason to believe that the customer was aware of them. In particular, the officer warned that refinancing would probably be necessary and could be impossible for the lender unless house prices continue to rise.*

There is no deception in Scenarios 4 and 5, because the lender did not cause the borrower to have a false belief. As for Scenario 3, we might again want to say *caveat emptor*, because buyers should take responsibility for themselves rather than relying on the seller to spell everything out. But we need an argument, not just an assertion.

It is helpful to look at the issue in general, since it comes up in all sales negotiation. The possibility of commerce as we know it requires a certain amount of trust between buyer and seller. In particular, the buyer must trust the seller to point out important facts about the product, particularly when the buyer is unlikely to be aware of them. Otherwise, the burden of trying to understand every product one buys would be too great. The seller, after all, is most familiar with the product. Similarly, the seller must trust buyers to choose a product that is right for them. Buyers are most familiar with their needs, and it is impractical for the seller to investigate the personal circumstances of every customer.

The seller's actions are ungeneralizable *if they presuppose a level of trust that would not exist if all sellers behaved similarly.* In Scenario 3, the seller was silent about a key risk factor that he or she had reason to believe the buyer misunderstood. Arguably, many subprime borrowers went ahead with their loans in such cases because they trusted the lender to exercise due diligence. They assumed the lender would raise any serious issues about their ability to repay. This trust would evaporate if lenders consistently failed to raise such issues. Borrowers would become wary of lenders, particularly as they come to realize that the loan originators lose nothing if the borrower defaults. Many would back away from a loan, which would defeat the lender's purpose. As it happened, many subprime lenders in fact failed to exercise due diligence. The subprime market collapsed, perhaps even before customer trust could evaporate, but this only demonstrates ungeneralizability for a second reason. The lender's action in Scenario 4, on the other hand, is probably generalizable, even though the lender failed to provide key information. If sellers always failed to provide key information when there is no reason to believe that buyers are uninformed, then commerce could still proceed. It may be less efficient than it is now, because sellers often volunteer such information, but efficiency is a utilitarian criterion and not the issue in a generalization test. What matters is that the level of trust could still be high enough to allow subprime mortgage loans to go through—or, strictly speaking, whether it is consistent with the seller's beliefs that the level of trust would be high enough under these circumstances.

On the other hand, it seems likely that Scenario 4 rarely, if ever, applied during the subprime mortgage frenzy. Lenders probably had reason to suspect that few customers fully appreciated the risk. This is particularly the case because the practice of repackaging loans was relatively new. Many customers were probably unaware that lenders no longer had a clear incentive to make sure that loans were well secured. The situation therefore reverts to Scenario 3, where a failure to point out the risk is unethical.

Even when the customer is aware of the risk, it may be unethical to *tempt* customers with this type of loan. Suppose the loan officer learns from experience that customers frequently take out subprime loans when they know it is too risky for them. They do it because they really want that house. Is it OK to offer such a person a subprime loan, knowing that the customer will probably make the wrong decision?

We discussed temptation in Case 6.4 and concluded that the issue boils down to a utilitarian test: Temptation is wrong if it reduces overall expected utility. Presenting subprime loans to customers could tempt them to take out loans they cannot repay and thereby do much harm. The harm is due to the borrower's own choices, but this is irrelevant to the utilitarian test. What matters is whether harm results from the loan. If tempting the customer reduces expected utility, the temptation is unethical. If we assume as before, however, that the subprime loans in question boost expected utility, the temptation is ethical.

## FORECLOSURE: UTILITARIAN TEST

As for the ethics of foreclosure, one might again argue that in typical cases the impact on the borrower dominates this utilitarian calculation. The alternative to foreclosure is to negotiate more favorable terms for the borrower. This may or may not be better for the company than foreclosure, but in typical cases, it is much better for the borrower. It is true that the borrower has already enjoyed a rent-free house for two years at low payments, and one may say that he/she "deserves" nothing more (whatever that means). But all this is irrelevant to the utilitarian calculation. Renegotiating the loan probably maximizes utility because it is better for the borrower, or if it doesn't, we need to understand why the borrower's marginal interests don't dominate the calculation. Now let's look at the other tests.

## FORECLOSURE: GENERALIZATION TEST

There is a seemingly obvious generalization argument that lenders should not give people a break when they can't make the payments. It would create moral hazard. If lenders always relaxed the repayment terms, borrowers would take out loans they can't afford.

This went by a little too quickly (as moral hazard arguments often do). The generalization test asks whether Countrywide would have been able to achieve the purpose of relaxing the terms if all lenders relaxed terms when borrowers can't pay.[12] Actually, one can imagine a mortgage loan industry in which lenders regularly relax the terms when necessary. It is true that, in this system, borrowers will "agree" to written terms they cannot meet. But everyone knows they are actually agreeing to the more favorable terms that will be negotiated if necessary. Everyone makes adjustments for this, and the system works.

However, Countrywide could not have achieved the *purpose* of relaxing the terms in this kind of system, and this is what counts for the generalization test. The purpose of relaxing the terms is to avoid foreclosure. If everyone relaxed the terms, then borrowers would have already anticipated easier terms, and borrowers in trouble would be unable to meet even these. So Countrywide wouldn't have been able to avoid foreclosure by relaxing the terms.[13] Thus the ethical problem is not simply moral hazard, but specifically the impossibility of achieving the purpose of renegotiating the loan if everyone did so when borrowers can't make the payments.

This argument shows that, at least under normal circumstances, it is not only permissible for lenders to get tough when borrowers can't pay, but they have an ethical obligation to do so. Renegotiating the loan passes the utilitarian test but not the generalization test.

However, renegotiation is permissible if the lender would benefit from renegotiating the loan, during a crisis or otherwise. This was the situation for many lenders, for whom foreclosure resulted in a major loss due to rock-bottom house prices. It is not unusual for parties to a contract to renegotiate when both would benefit, and no one raises eyebrows about this. Why are mortgage loans any different? Probably they aren't. If all lenders regularly renegotiated loans when both lender and borrower would benefit, the lenders would still benefit. There is no reason to suppose that borrowers would take on too much risk, on the chance that it would benefit the lender to renegotiate the terms. So renegotiation is permissible if it would benefit both parties and is therefore obligatory because it maximizes utility.

One might argue that renegotiation is permissible in extraordinary situations like a financial crisis, even if it doesn't benefit the lender. This seems generalizable, because most borrowers wouldn't anticipate easier terms in cases of financial hardship, if loans were negotiated only in times of crisis. But we must carefully examine the reason for renegotiation before testing for generalizability. One possible reason is that it benefits the lender, but we have already acknowledged that renegotiation is permissible in this case. If it doesn't benefit the lender, then a possible reason is simply that it increases utility. But renegotiation would increase utility whether or not it is a time of crisis. The lender has no apparent rationale for renegotiating in one case and not in the other. If the government incentivizes renegotiation, as in fact has occurred, then this could provide a rationale—either because the incentives make renegotiation in the lender's interest or because the company wants to create positive public image by showing cooperation during a crisis. But in these cases, the company renegotiates because it benefits the company, which we have judged to be permissible. If the lender has received government bailout money or subsidies, this may carry a legal or ethical obligation to restructure loans.

Let's now examine whether it is permissible for the lender to foreclose if it deceived the borrower about the risk of the loan (Scenarios 1 and 2) or acted unethically for some other reason (Scenario 3). Opponents of foreclosure claim that these circumstances call for flexibility in working with the borrower.

If deception was involved in negotiating the loan contract (Scenarios 1 and 2), one might argue that the contract is void. There is a similar principle in the law. From an ethical point of view, a contract clearly requires mutual consent. If one party deceives the other about the nature of the product being sold, we can argue that there is no mutual consent and no contract.

However, this is not what happened in Scenarios 1 and 2. The lender deceived the customer about the risk, and the risk was a key element in deciding whether to take out the loan, but the terms of the loan itself were clear and mutually understood. It is just that the lender deceived the borrower about the advisability of taking out the loan. However unethical it may be to deceive the customer, the deception does not nullify the contract, from an ethical point of view. The same point applies even more strongly in Scenarios 3 and 4, where there was no deception.

There is one possible situation that voids the contract, however:

- *Scenario 1a. The lender led the borrower to believe that the lender would renegotiate the loan after two years (and that there is no risk that it would not). The possibility of renegotiation could therefore be interpreted as part of the contract.*

In this scenario, the lender genuinely deceived the borrower about the product being sold, and there was no mutual consent. There was no contract and therefore no contractual obligation. A particular law court may not care to recognize this fact and may order the borrower to pay under the original terms, but the fact remains that there was no contract from an ethical point of view, and the lender should voluntarily restructure the loan in a way that maximizes overall utility.

The same applies if the loan originator sold the mortgage to a third party, which is the usual situation. The originator sold a contract that is not a contract. The sale may have been unethical and the purchaser (assignee) may have a right to compensation from the originator. Yet the fact remains that the borrower is not bound by a valid contract, and the loan purchaser is ethically obligated to settle the matter in a way that maximizes total utility.

We have found that the loan contract is binding in Scenarios 1–5 but not in Scenario 1a. This means that in Scenarios 1–5, the borrower is ethically obligated to repay the complete loan, or surrender the house. It does not necessarily follow, however, that the lender can ethically foreclose on the loan—that is, compel the borrower to surrender the house through legal process. If the lender would benefit from renegotiation, there is an obligation to renegotiate, because it maximizes utility and is generalizable.

## JUST COMPENSATION

Even if the lender wouldn't benefit from renegotiation, we can ask whether the lender owes the client some kind of restitution to *compensate* for the deceptive or unethical behavior in Scenarios 1–3 and 1a. This compensation could take the form of renegotiating the loan or postponing some payments, rather than foreclosing. After all, the lender's behavior harmed the client. We have a strong intuition that if we harm someone, particularly through unethical conduct, then we ought to make up for it somehow. The entire law of torts is based on this idea.

Just compensation is tricky to analyze, however. We probably have a strong intuition on this topic because we are accustomed to legal remedies. It may in fact be good *social policy* for the law to require people to compensate those they harm, because this deters harmful acts and thereby increases utility. But social policy is not the issue before us. The issue is what an individual mortgage lender's policy should be. So we ask whether failure to compensate violates a condition of rational choice.

We have already found that failure to compensate in Scenarios 1–5 passes the generalization test, because foreclosure (without compensation) passes the test. However, the utilitarian principle seems to require compensation, at least if the borrower is financially distressed. Due to the concavity of utility functions mentioned earlier, compensating financially distressed borrowers in Scenarios 1–5 would create more utility for the borrowers than it would lose for the lenders. Yet this doesn't explain why a company should help out victims *of its own* deception rather than victims of someone else's deception, or both. The utilitarian argument doesn't justify *compensation* in the sense of making up for one's own wrongdoing. Again, it may be good for the law to require it, and a company should compensate when required by law.[14] Yet utilitarian and generalization arguments don't require compensation from the lenders simply on the basis that they are the perpetrators of the damage.

## VIRTUE ETHICS

The actions of loan officers should be consistent with who they are as professionals. Presumably, the mission of a mortgage loan officer is to make home ownership possible. Subprime loans, properly designed and administered, are entirely consistent with this mission because they help more people to own a home. It is hard to believe, however, that a 2/28 loan could be designed with the goal of making home ownership possible. Rather, it seems designed to entice borrowers with unnaturally low payments up front. A loan officer concerned with promoting home ownership should offer realistic loan products that help the client work toward a good credit rating.

In particular, a loan officer should not make a loan when there is a substantial risk of foreclosure, because this obviously frustrates the mission of the profession. We have already found that subprime loans are unethical in Scenarios 1–3. If loan officers avoid making subprime loans in these situations and recommend the loans only when they maximize the borrower's utility, then they will probably act consistently with their mission.

We have so far found no obligation for a loan officer to warn customers that refinancing may be impossible, if there is no particular reason to believe that the customer is unaware of this. It is unclear whether virtue ethics imposes an obligation of this sort, because it is not obviously part of the loan officer's professional role. The situation is different for a financial advisor, or a real estate broker that is working for the buyer. Real estate brokers have in fact been criticized for abdicating their responsibility in this area. Perhaps they do so because, in the peculiar U.S. system, brokers advising the buyer are typically paid by the seller and have an incentive to push up the house price—a situation that clearly requires ethical examination.

One can argue, however, that virtue ethics requires some kind of compensation in Scenarios 1–3, perhaps in the form of a renegotiated loan. Virtue ethics is vague and generally does not justify precise courses of action. But if the loan officer's mission is to assist people to finance their own home, then it makes no sense for the loan officers to forget about their clients after deceiving them or otherwise unethically inducing them to sign the wrong loan. They should want to correct their mistakes and put their clients back on the path to home ownership. This could include renegotiation, which is generalizable in Scenarios 1–3 if done to fulfill a professional duty that is not yet fulfilled. Loan officers would still be able to complete their duty in this fashion if all lenders did likewise.

The problem is that practically none of the troubled loans are still held by the mortgage companies that made them, because they were sold off. The loan officers can claim that the matter is out of their hands. It is hard to argue that the current owners of the mortgages have a professional duty to correct the mistakes of the loan originators, particularly when they often don't know which loans were negotiated in an unethical manner.

## CONCLUSION

Subprime lending can be perfectly ethical under the right circumstances. However, if making a subprime loan creates less *expected* utility than not making it, the loan is unethical. Because the utility calculation is dominated by the customer's welfare, a loan that reduces expected utility for the borrower is unethical.

If the loan results in greater expected utility for the borrower, it may be ethical even if the downside risk is large. The loan terms should be crafted to maximize utility for the borrower, however. The harsh 2/28 scheme and similar plans don't qualify, because they may force many borrowers to refinance after a few years—which may be impossible if real estate prices drop.

In addition, the ethics of subprime lending depends on exactly how the lender interacts with its customers. It is unethical to say or do anything that leads customers to believe that they can *count on* the possibility of refinancing to reduce large payments in the future. If the lender has reason to believe that the customer misunderstands the risk of being unable to refinance, then the lender should clearly explain the risk.

If there is no particular reason to believe that the customer is unaware of the risk, then there is no obligation to point it out. However, one might argue that during the heyday of subprime lending, there was almost always a reason to believe that the customer didn't fully appreciate the risk.

Renegotiating an ethically valid subprime loan contract is neither obligatory nor permissible, unless it would benefit both borrower and lender. The contract is ethically valid even if the lender deceived the borrower about the risk, although the deception is itself unethical. However, if both borrower and lender would benefit from renegotiation, then renegotiation is obligatory. In addition, if the loan originator still holds a loan that was made without full discussion of the risk, virtue ethics requires the lender to make some sort of effort to compensate the borrower. Compensation can take the form of renegotiation for the purpose of fulfilling the lender's professional duty to its clients. There is also an ethical duty to compensate when required by law.

In addition, if the lender led customers to believe that they could count on the possibility of refinancing *through the lender*, then the loan contract is void for ethical purposes. The mortgage owner, whether the originator or not, is obligated to renegotiate payments in a way that maximizes overall utility.

The ethical landscape is complicated, and these conclusions are summarized in Table 6.1.

The design of public policy to deal with the subprime crisis, regulate future lending, and govern financial markets pose further issues that are not addressed here. There may be an ethical obligation for the government to work with lenders to rescue borrowers, provide greater oversight of financial markets, or restructure the financial system. ■

| TABLE 6.1 | Ethical evaluation of subprime lending, foreclosure, and renegotiation |

| Action | Pass Utilitarian Test? | Pass Generalization Test? | Pass Virtue Ethics Test?* | Pass all the Tests? |
|---|---|---|---|---|
| *Subprime lending* | **Yes**, if the *expected* net benefit for the borrower is positive, and in particular the loans are properly designed (e.g., no 2/28 loans) | **Yes**, in Scenarios 4–5** <br> **No**, in Scenarios 1–3 and 1a | **Yes**, in Scenarios 4–5, if expected net benefit for the borrower is positive. <br> **No**, in Scenarios 1–3 and 1a, or if expected net benefit for the borrower is negative | **Yes**, in Scenarios 4–5, if expected net benefit for the borrower is positive <br> **No**, in Scenarios 1–3 and 1a, or if expected net benefit for the borrower is negative |
| *Foreclosure* | **Yes**, if renegotiating fails generalization test <br> **No**, otherwise | **Yes**, in Scenarios 1–5, unless renegotiation benefits the lender <br> **No**, in Scenario 1a, or if renegotiation benefits the lender | **Yes** | **Yes**, in Scenarios 1–5, unless renegotiation benefits the lender <br> **No**, in Scenario 1a, or if renegotiation benefits the lender |
| *Renegotiation* | **Yes** | **Yes**, in Scenario 1a, or if renegotiation benefits the lender <br> **No**, in Scenarios 1–5, or unless renegotiation benefits the lender | **Yes** | **Yes**, in Scenario 1a, or if renegotiation benefits the lender <br> **No**, in Scenarios 1–5, or unless renegotiation benefits the lender |

*It is assumed that the loan originator no longer owns the mortgage. Otherwise, the lender has obligations as discussed in the text.

**Arguably, Scenario 4 rarely occurred during the heyday of subprime lending.

## CASE 6.6

# Super Size Me

SYNOPSIS[15]

The documentary film *Super Size Me* examines whether McDonald's restaurants cause obesity and other unhealthy conditions. The director Morgan Spurlock eats nothing but McDonald's food for a month, while three physicians monitor the effect on his body. He eats jumbo portions when asked if he wants to "Super Size it." He also restricts his exercise during this period to something close to the U.S. average.

Spurlock reports that, during the month, he added 24 pounds to his starting weight of 185 pounds. Blood tests revealed substantially higher cholesterol levels and adverse effects on his liver. Spurlock also reported lethargy, depression, and heart palpitations during the period, perhaps in part because he was worried about possible long-term damage to his health.

The film also examines the rise in U.S. obesity levels; the nutritional content of processed food; McDonald's marketing strategy toward children; the role of schools in providing sugary soft drinks, French fries, and other junk food; views of the U.S. Surgeon General; and the response of the fast-food lobby. Spurlock was unable to obtain an interview with McDonald's representatives. McDonald's removed the Super Size option from its menu shortly before the film was released, although the company denied that it did so in response to the film.

After his McDonald's binge, Spurlock went on a "detox" diet designed by his vegan girlfriend. He lost 20 of the extra pounds in five months and the remaining four pounds in nine additional months.

## THE ETHICAL ISSUES

The main ethical issue raised in the film is whether McDonald's is doing something wrong by selling and promoting its menu of fast food. Other issues include whether schools should serve junk food; whether the government should regulate fast food, require clearer labeling, or restrict how junk food is marketed to children; and whether obese plaintiffs who sue McDonald's should win compensation. We will focus on McDonald's ethical obligations, because this is enough to keep us thinking for a long time. It also raises a basic issue for marketing: Is it ethical to sell products that customers sometimes misuse or overuse, resulting in harm?

The basic case against McDonald's is that its food is unhealthy, and it is unethical so sell products that harm the customer. Defenders of McDonald's respond that (a) no one is forced to eat hamburgers and French fries, (b) consenting adults should have the right to eat what they want, and besides, (c) McDonald's offers salads. Critics respond that McDonald's entices children into its restaurants with play areas and kids meals in order to hook them on unhealthy food. Defenders reply that parents are responsible for their children and should take them somewhere else if they don't like McDonald's practices. The debate never gets far above this level, and nothing is resolved. Let's see if we can make some progress on the issue by applying the conditions of rational choice.

## UTILITARIAN TEST

Let's assume, for the sake of argument, that McDonald's menu and marketing techniques cause greater harm than would result if McDonald's changed its ways. Whether this is really true is a

question of fact and cannot be resolved by ethical analysis. Yet it seems reasonable, and in any case, we should explore the ethical consequences if it is true.

This is a rather weak assumption. We are not supposing that McDonald's is the cause of or even a major contributor to obesity, as suggested by the film. We propose only that McDonald's could make a more positive contribution to society than it is making now by making at least marginal changes to its menu or marketing approach.

On the other hand, we are not simply assuming that McDonald's food is unhealthy. It is conceivable that McDonald's could increase net utility by selling unhealthy food, perhaps because its customers would not overindulge, and the pleasure of eating a few Big Macs would outweigh the negative health effects. Rather, we are supposing that greater net overall utility would result if McDonald's sold and promoted healthier food.

Given this assumption, McDonald's fails the utilitarian test—unless selling healthier food or changing its marketing techniques would violate some other condition for rational choice, such as the generalization test. We will examine this possibility in a moment, but let's suppose for the moment that it doesn't and see where this gets us.

It brings us to the inevitable conclusion that McDonald's conduct is unethical. It is true that customers freely choose to eat hamburgers and French fries, but this is irrelevant to the utilitarian test. If McDonald's menu and marketing techniques result in free customer choices that cause more net harm than if they chose otherwise, then utility is not maximized. It doesn't matter whether customers make a free choice, whether they are aware or should be aware of the health risks, whether they are adults or children, or whether parents should be responsible for their children. All that matters is the total utility that results.

This may seem to demand too much from McDonald's. Profit-making firms can't afford to behave like welfare agencies. If they are required to maximize social good, they will go broke. Perhaps, but the utilitarian calculation takes account of this. If offering healthier food would drive McDonald's out of business, and if this would result in less net overall utility, then its unhealthy food passes the utilitarian test. If going out of business would result in *more* net utility, then McDonald's *should* go out of business. No company that does more harm than good should exist.

We are not assuming, however, that McDonald's does more harm than good. We are only assuming that it could create more utility by modifying its menu or marketing strategy, taking into account any effect this may have on its profitability.

## GENERALIZATION TEST

Many defenders of McDonald's worry that if all businesses self-regulated in the way that critics ask McDonald's to self-regulate, we would lose our freedom. We would live in a dreary Soviet-like society where all choices are made for us.

This has the flavor of a generalization test, which states that the reason for an action should be consistent with the assumption that everyone with the same reason acts the same way. It is not really a generalization test, however, because the test doesn't ask whether generalization would result in a better world. It only asks whether the results of generalization would be consistent with the reasons for the action.

It is true that the *reason* for changing the McDonald's menu is to make the world better, and we can apply the generalization test to this reason. As it happens, the reason passes the test. Selling healthier food would continue to make the world better if all businesses sold a product line that maximizes utility. Perhaps it wouldn't make the world better if other businesses sold only *healthy* products. In such a boring world, removing the few remaining unhealthy products (McDonald's hamburgers and French fries) could create enough additional misery to offset improved health. But there is no reason to believe that every business must restrict itself to healthy products to maximize utility. A Mom and Pop candy store arguably maximizes utility by selling sinfully luscious fudge brownies rather than celery sticks. This results only in an occasional indulgence for customers, and the pleasure probably outweighs the small fat and cholesterol deposits that result. McDonald's is different, because its prominence in the market leads too many people to indulge too often, or so we are assuming. Its menu is a victim of its own success.

So a world in which all businesses maximize utility need not be a dreary Soviet-like society at all. There could be plenty of temptations to make bad choices. It is just that people would yield to temptation less often than in a society in which businesses are like McDonald's.

## MARKETING TO CHILDREN

The issue of marketing to children has had little relevance to the analysis so far. If McDonald's menu and marketing techniques fail the utilitarian test, as I have argued, then its behavior is unethical whether or not children are involved.

However, the ethics of marketing to children may become relevant when McDonald's reforms its behavior. Let's suppose that the company puts appealing, healthy food on the menu and conspicuously warns customers about the nutritional content of its burgers and fries. As a result, customers only occasionally order junk food, just enough to maximize pleasure without compromising their health. The play areas provide a place where kids can get healthy exercise while under the supervision of parents (as already claimed by McDonald's corporate PR). The company continues to target kids with advertising that induces them to nag their parents to take them to McDonald's, but we will suppose that even this adds to net

utility because many of these kids get more exercise than they otherwise would.

However, let's suppose that *some* kids are not so lucky. They don't exercise, and their parents let them eat all the burgers and fries they want. So they continue to get fat. We want to know if it is wrong for McDonald's to manipulate these kids, even though it is maximizing net utility (due to all the other kids who get more exercise). It is perhaps unlikely that McDonald's could really maximize utility in this way, but let's suppose it could.

The typical response to this kind of dilemma is that it is OK to entice consenting adults with harmful foods, but not children. But nothing in our ethical toolbox supports this idea. Tempting people is wrong if it results in less utility, whether they are consenting adults or not. As for the kids, we set up the scenario so that McDonald's is already maximizing utility, which means there can be no utilitarian objection to tempting them with unhealthy food. We have to find some other ground for objection. We might argue that manipulating kids in this way is roughly analogous to slipping a drug into Mom's coffee that makes her crave Big Macs, because kids are naïve and don't see what is going on. It is a violation of autonomy, which is normally ungeneralizable. But if violation of autonomy is the problem, we have to say that manipulating kids *for any reason* is wrong. For example, a manipulative marketing campaign that induces kids to eat their broccoli would be wrong—or, to push the issue harder, a campaign that inspires them to do their homework. So the typical response again misses the point. It is not harmfulness of the food that makes it wrong to entice the kids, but the manipulative nature of the enticement.

Even this is hard to defend. We say it is all right for *parents* to manipulate their children, because children aren't ready for autonomy and need guidance, but it is not all right for a corporation to do it. Why? If it is merely because parental guidance is better for the kids or society than corporate guidance, then the argument is utilitarian, and there is nothing wrong with corporate manipulation of kids if the net outcome is positive. One can argue that manipulating kids is unethical for other reasons, and we will examine that case in a moment, but we can already say one thing for sure. The common notion that tempting adults with harmful products is OK, but tempting kids is not, is indefensible and useless as a guideline.

## UNDERMINING PARENTS

One problem with manipulating children through marketing campaigns is that it undermines parental influence. Kids in the United States spend more than 20 hours a week in front of computer and TV screens and are exposed to countless promotional messages, not only in ads but in the programming itself. Some marketing firms interview kids to find out what kind of nagging techniques are most effective with their parents, and then demonstrate these techniques in ads. In theory, parents can take away the screens and ignore the nagging. But forbidding screens is a draconian measure in our day and age. The creation of frivolous desires substitutes corporate persuasion for parental guidance and reduces the ability of parents to transmit their values to their kids.

The problem with this is that our society assigns parents and guardians primary responsibility for raising their children. No other person or institution is willing or able to take on this burden, aside from orphanages and juvenile detention centers in special cases (and it's not clear that they are able). But parents cannot be held responsible for raising their kids if outside forces constantly frustrate their efforts. If corporate advertisers were willing to assume parental responsibility, then their interference could be tolerated, but they are not willing.

Manipulative children's marketing therefore appears to fail the generalization test, if it is intrusive enough. It assumes that children have a caregiver they can nag but refuses to take on a caregiver's responsibilities. If its policy of interfering with parental guidance were generalized, there would be no effective caregiver unless the marketers themselves were willing to take on this role, which they are not. In a nutshell, manipulative marketing that is sufficiently aggressive would, if generalized, undermine the family structure on which it relies for its effectiveness.

This does not mean that it is always unethical for institutions outside the family to interfere with parental guidance. For example, a government that requires childhood education can pass the generalization test if it is willing to take commensurate responsibility for raising children, in this case by providing high-quality education. But aggressive corporate marketing firms are unwilling and ill-equipped to take on child care responsibilities that are commensurate with the degree to which they intrude in family life.

## CONCLUSION

If one assumes that McDonald's could create more net utility by changing its menu or its marketing techniques, taking into account any financial effect on the corporation, then its behavior is unethical. It makes no difference whether the company is marketing to consenting adults or to children, whether it currently offers salads, or whether parents are exercising their responsibility. It doesn't matter whether McDonald's is a major cause of obesity. All that matters is that McDonald's could have at least a marginally more positive impact by changing its approach.

The truth or falsehood of this assumption is a question of fact that must be resolved by empirical investigation, not by ethical reasoning. Yet the assumption seems reasonable, and in any case, McDonald's cannot know that its current behavior is ethical unless it determines that there is no clear evidence for the truth of the assumption.

McDonald's obligations in this area are likely to be different from those of many other food vendors, due to its dominant position in the industry. Even if the McDonald's menu is unethical, this does not imply that unhealthy menus in other establishments are necessarily unethical. Nor is self-regulation by McDonald's in this area inconsistent with freedom of choice.

The common notion that it is permissible to tempt consenting adults with harmful products, but not children, is indefensible and useless as an ethical guideline.

Marketing techniques that manipulate children in a sufficiently intrusive way are unethical, regardless of whether they maximize utility.

---

## CASE 6.7

# Conoco's "Green" Oil Strategy

### SYNOPSIS[16]

In the late 1980s, Conoco, a division of DuPont, began to investigate the possibility of drilling for oil in the Ecuadorian rain forest. Conoco held 35% of a consortium formed for this purpose that included several smaller oil companies. Although Ecuador produces relatively little oil by world standards, its output is crucial for the country's economy. The national oil company Petroecuador would receive 80% of the profits earned by the consortium, after the investment cost was recovered. Conoco focused on "Block 16," where test drills showed significant oil reserves.

However, previous drilling in this region had created environmental and cultural problems. Seventeen million gallons of oil had been spilled, four million gallons of hazardous waste dumped into rivers every day, and unknown amounts of toxic drilling mud

buried. Access roads allowed landless peasants to settle and clear large areas of the forest, initially with government encouragement. This in turn threatened the extraordinary biodiversity of the region. Although Block 16 lay almost entirely within Yasuni National Park, it was difficult to keep settlers out. In particular, the increased access and activity in the region threatened the unique culture of the Huaorani people, one of the world's few traditional societies that had been little affected by outside contact. The Sierra Club Legal Defense Fund accused oil companies of "ethnocide" for their disruption of the culture.

To deal with these issues, Conoco drew up a plan that would minimize environmental damage, at a cost of increasing the investment by 5–10%. It was justified to stockholders on the grounds that if Conoco were required to add environmental controls later, the cost could be much greater. The plan called for the collection and treatment of oil runoff and hazardous wastes, and the reuse and safe deposit of drilling mud. Encroachment on the area would be restricted by posting guards and accessing it via ferries rather than bridges built across the Rio Napo. Employees would be forbidden from trading with the Huaorani or fishing on their land, and so forth. In 1990, Conoco convened a meeting at which it presented its plan to environmental and other interested groups.[17]

## THE ISSUES

The issues in this case are fundamental. What are a private corporation's obligations to protect the environment, over and above what is required by law? What are its obligations to protect indigenous cultures?

The *government's* duty to protect the environment is not the issue before us. People often say that environmental protection is the government's responsibility and therefore not the responsibility of private business. The problem here is with the "therefore." Environmental protection may well be the government's responsibility, but this does not imply that business has no responsibility, particularly when the government does not act. The obligations of business must be addressed directly. We will do so by applying the conditions of rational choice.

## UTILITARIAN TEST

The utilitarian test is straightforward, at least in principle. If polluting the environment does more harm to more people than not polluting, then it is wrong. Pollution controls may not maximize utility for the company and its stockholders, but this is a different matter. Typically, the cost of pollution to all concerned is not fully reflected in costs to the corporation. Unfortunately, it is difficult to determine whether the overall benefits of a given level of pollution—cheap energy for consumers, revenue for Ecuador, profit for stockholders, and so forth—exceed the overall costs. This is a question of fact, not ethics. It requires environmental and economic analysis, which we cannot conduct here. Ethical analysis tells us what to do once the facts are in.

Conoco executives may protest that they have a fiduciary duty to maximize profit for the owners, within the law. Legally dumping waste into the river may be the way to maximize profit. The issue here, however, is what the *corporation* should do; that is, what its owners should do. If it is ethical for the owners to pollute, then presumably it is ethical for their executives to do it for them.

Conoco owners may protest that even if pollution does more harm than good, they must compete with firms that have no scruples about pollution. If Conoco pays for pollution controls, the competition will force them out of Ecuador. Then some other firm will pollute anyway. So, on balance, Conoco can maximize utility by polluting as much as necessary to keep the firm in business. This results in no

greater pollution than would occur anyway, and it avoids the adjustment costs incurred by employees who are laid off.

One often hears the comment, "if I don't do it, somebody else will." We discussed this response in Case 4.5 and concluded that, if true, it shows at most that the action in question is consistent with the utilitarian principle. It doesn't show that the actions satisfies the other conditions for rational choice, and therefore doesn't show it is ethical.

In the present case, it seems reasonable that if Conoco doesn't do it, some other company will. We therefore conclude that pollution *to the extent necessary to stay in business* passes the utilitarian test. Apparently, in Conoco's case, not much pollution is necessary to stay in business, because the company is seriously proposing an aggressive cleanup effort. If Conoco can survive with a clean operation, and if a clean operation generates more utility on balance than a dirty one, then the utilitarian test says that Conoco must have a clean operation.

## GENERALIZATION TEST

Let's suppose for the sake of argument, however, that a significant amount of pollution is necessary to keep Conoco in business in Ecuador. Does this level of pollution pass the other tests for rational choice, such as the generalization test?

An analogy may be useful at this point. Analogical reasoning cannot settle ethical issues, but it can help direct one's attention to the relevant arguments. Suppose I decide to dump my garbage on the property next door. We can suppose the dumping passes the utilitarian test, because the garbage causes equal harm whether it is on my property or next door. Yet something seems wrong about burdening someone else with my garbage.

At the most elementary level, it is a violation of property rights. But exactly what property rights do people have? For example, is the use of eminent domain to obtain land for highways a violation of property rights? To answer these questions, we end up going back to the basic conditions of rational choice, and so we may as well start there.

Spoiling someone else's property, solely for my own convenience, is normally unethical because it is ungeneralizable—even when it results in no net less loss of utility. The reason is that the whole point of my action is to spoil *someone else's* property rather than *my* property. So I cannot accomplish my aim unless the institution of property exists. However, if people always defaced another's property whenever it is convenient, there would be no institution of property. The purpose of owning property is to have some control over it and to prevent people from doing whatever they want to it. There would be no point in buying or owning property if no one respected it.

If Conoco dumps oil or hazardous wastes on someone else's property, then this is clearly ungeneralizable and unethical. Block 16 is presumably some else's property because it is part of a national park and therefore belongs to the government of Ecuador.

Conoco might argue that it has permission to pollute Block 16, because the government has imposed no regulations. Defacing another's property with permission seems clearly generalizable.

It is not so obvious that Conoco actually has permission to pollute Block 16, but let's grant that it does. The larger issue concerns pollution damage to the region as a whole. Dumping wastes on neighboring property is unethical, and Conoco is acting unethically if it is doing this. Yet what can we say about more general pollution of the environment, such as rivers, groundwater, the air, and so forth? Is this an infringement of property rights?

Again, the test is whether the institution of property would survive in a form that makes it possible for Conoco to achieve its purposes if companies regularly fouled the earth whenever it suited their purpose. Perhaps it would. Pollution was rampant in the early days of the Industrial Revolution, to the point of transforming some areas into hellholes that were scarcely inhabitable. Yet property was still being bought and sold. It is therefore hard to make an ethical case against general environmental pollution on the basis of property rights.

Even if generalizing pollution does not undermine the institution of property, perhaps it undermines Conoco's purposes in a broader sense. There is a reason that the sort of pollution oil companies practice in Ecuador is illegal in Europe and North America. It is because this level of pollution may be incompatible with the first-world infrastructure that makes a company like Conoco possible. The purpose behind Conoco's pollution is higher profits, but if everyone in the world polluted this much, business would be less profitable, due to the degraded environment and the depressed economy that would result. This was perhaps untrue in the nineteenth century, when the total potential for pollution was much smaller. But it may be true today. If so, generalizing Conoco's behavior defeats the purpose of the behavior, and the generalization test is failed.

Western companies sometimes adopt practices in third-world countries that are illegal at home. This has been criticized on the ground that it is hypocritical or inconsistent. Yet such comments prove little. The proper test is whether a company's purposes would be undermined if companies always behaved in the same way. In the case of Ecuador, past practices of oil companies may fail the test.

## ETHNOCIDE?

A century ago, the dominant view in the United States was that indigenous peoples should be absorbed into Western culture. The Carlisle Indian School in Pennsylvania was the first U.S. school established to do just this. It required native children to wear European clothes, speak English, and forget about their traditional culture. It was for their own good. Today, there are strong indigenous people's movements worldwide, which maintain that traditional cultures are intrinsically valuable and should be protected. Who is right?

A utilitarian analysis can easily accommodate the idea that distinctive cultures are intrinsically valuable. But the logic of

utilitarianism does not *require* this in any obvious way. Perhaps we can argue that it is inconsistent to value one's own culture but not another, but it would take some time and reflection to develop such an argument.

Even if we could establish that Conoco should value Huaorani culture for its own sake, there is no utilitarian imperative for Conoco to try to protect the culture if doing so would allow an uncaring competitor to replace Conoco. Naturally, if extinction of Huaorani culture reduces the well-being of these people in more conventional ways (wealth, happiness, etc.) without a compensating rise in utility elsewhere, then the utilitarian test requires Conoco to protect the culture—not for its own sake, but for the sake of the people in it.

Perhaps the generalization test, however, can require Conoco to protect an indigenous culture. Is ethnocide ethically equivalent to homicide? As viewed in the classical Western tradition, it is not. Homicide is ungeneralizable and wrong because it destroys agency. Ethnocide does not destroy individuals, on the traditional Western view, and therefore does not destroy agency.

However, this traditional view may be mistaken in supposing that agency is always exercised by individuals. Many cultures are communal, meaning that humans do not exist apart from their membership in a group, such as the family or community. In these cultures, one might argue that a community is an agent in the same sense that an individual is an agent in the Western worldview. Ethnocide therefore becomes murder.

A related line of argument is that one's culture defines to a great extent who one is. One who converts to a radically different culture literally becomes someone else. A biography[18] of an aboriginal Australian named Waipuldanya recounts how he spent part of his life in an isolated indigenous community but was later converted to Western culture by missionaries. In interviews with the biographer, Waipuldanya spoke of his former life as that of a different person. If this view is correct, replacing someone's culture with a radically different one is a form of murder.

These viewpoints represent new frontiers for Western ethics that are likely to be explored in coming years.

## VIRTUE ETHICS

I recently had some conversations with two managers in a major electric power company. It soon became clear that they and their colleagues view their work not just as a job but as an opportunity to make a contribution. They didn't see themselves as corporate villains who pollute the world. They see them themselves as making life better by providing energy that everyone wants, including their critics, while minimizing pollution.

Their company may not minimize pollution, but I wish to make a different point. These managers define who they are in part by their mission at work. To be consistent, they must not only maximize utility by producing clean power, but they must shape their lives around this imperative. These are not the same. If they stepped aside and let someone else do their jobs, utility could still be maximized. Utilitarian consistency does not require them to produce clean power as long as someone else does it equally well. But their definition of who they are requires them to occupy their own working lives with this mission.

Similarly, the people at Conoco might view themselves as having a mission of making life better with energy. Excessive pollution makes life worse and is therefore inconsistent with this mission. If excessive pollution is necessary to do business competitively in Ecuador, then from a utilitarian point of view they might as well stay in business, because the next company will be just as dirty. But from the viewpoint of virtue ethics, this is inconsistent with who they are. They should get out of Ecuador, even though their departure has no effect on the situation there. The criterion is not whether they "feel bad" about polluting, because we sometimes feel bad about doing the right thing. The criterion is a logical one, whether their actions are consistent with who they are.

This is an instance, by the way, in which the duties of owners and manager must be analyzed separately. The owners may be holders of mutual funds who don't even know what their money is doing. Perhaps they should know, but the point here is that the virtue ethics argument may not apply to them in the way it applies to managers who have built a career around producing energy.

## CONCLUSION

It has been a long argument, and the conclusion is a little complicated. Welcome to the real world.

Conoco's environmental policy passes the utilitarian test if its pollution level is, at most, the greater of (a) the minimum amount of pollution that allows Conoco to operate cheaply enough to stay in business in Ecuador and (b) the amount of pollution that results in the greatest net benefit created by Conoco's operations in Ecuador. The case description suggests that both (a) and (b) are much less than the typical pollution level of oil companies operating in the country.

There is no clear utilitarian argument that Conoco must protect indigenous cultures for their own sake. Conoco must of course consider the welfare of the individuals in the cultures, and it must protect these cultures if their extinction would result in a net decrease in overall wealth or happiness.

If Conoco passes the utilitarian test, it nonetheless fails the generalization test if it dumps pollution on property belonging to others, without their permission. It also fails the test if its pollution of rivers, ground water, and so forth is great enough that if all companies polluted to this degree, the world economy would be degraded to the point that Conoco could no longer benefit financially from the lack of pollution controls. Thus Conoco probably fails the test if its pollution is significantly greater than that allowed by law in first-world nations.

There are reasonable arguments that the generalization test imposes obligations to protect indigenous cultures for their own sake. However, this issue lies on the frontier of ethical theory and requires more exploration.

Finally, virtue ethics suggests that career oil executives may have an obligation to get out of Ecuador if economic survival there requires significant pollution, even if their departure has no net effect on the pollution level. This specific obligation may not apply to the owners or stockholders of the firm.

In summary, Conoco should reduce its pollution to a level substantially less than that of oil companies previously operating in Ecuador, if this allows it to stay in business there. If staying in business requires a pollution level significantly greater than that allowed by law in Europe and North America, it should get out of Ecuador in any case. Its executives may have an obligation to get out even if a lower level of pollution is possible. ▤

## Exercises

1. *Too much pressure.*[19] Hank Kolb was put in charge of quality assurance at a plant where practices were not up to par. The most immediate issue facing him was what to do about some pressurized cans of lubricant that had just been shipped out. The cans had been overpressurized by faulty equipment. When this was discovered, one of the production supervisors vented the excess by hand without taking measurements to make sure the pressure was within tolerances. One option was to recall the cans and check them systematically, but this would be an expensive and time-consuming process, and it would antagonize customers. Should Kolb recall the cans?

   *Hints.* See Case 6.2 for guidance on how to analyze this case. The utilitarian test can perhaps be applied by the use of statistical sampling to estimate the cost of possible injuries. Kolb could recall a random sample of the cans for this purpose. However, you must ask whether statistical sampling alone can enable Kolb to promise safety, as required by the generalization principle, or whether a complete recall is necessary. Statistical sampling presupposes that uncontrolled defects are random.

2. *Fraud at Interspeed Corporation.*[20] Interspeed Corporation had just gone public, and Senior Vice-President for Sales Arthur Goodwin was keen to meet annual revenue targets. The fourth quarter target, for example, was $3 million, but the books showed only $1.9 in revenue. Goodwin decided he had to do something. He persuaded Solunet Inc. to take delivery of $1.2 million in inventory and hold it until another Interspeed customer bought it shortly after the new year began. Solunet was allowed to return the goods to InterSpeed if it couldn't sell them to the third party. Goodwin counted the $1.2 million as revenue and so pushed fourth-quarter revenue to $3.1 million, slightly above the target. Goodwin's conduct was a clear violation of GAAP. Solunet didn't actually buy the goods, because it didn't commit itself to paying for them. So there was no revenue to report.

As it turned out, the customer Goodwin counted on wouldn't buy the inventory. So Goodwin arranged for another company, I-Way, to buy or lease the equipment. When I-Way could not come up with the money, Goodwin transferred funds to I-Way, which leased the goods from a leasing agent. The leasing agent bought the goods from Solunet, which used the money to pay Interspeed, completing the circle.

Goodwin kept digging himself into a hole. In another incident, he forged a signature on an altered contract to create the impression that Interspeed had made a $6.4 million sale. Before it was all over, he had overstated the company's revenues by 60%, or $9 million. In a June 2006 Federal jury trial, Goodwin was convicted of securities fraud for his activities at Interspeed. He was sentenced to 30 months in jail, followed by a three-year supervised release. The Securities and Exchange Commission (SEC) also brought a civil action against Goodwin for the same offenses. In May 2007, he settled with the SEC by agreeing never to serve as an officer or director of a public corporation and by turning over $100,521 in earnings that resulted from his fraud. The payment was waived on grounds of financial hardship.

It doesn't take rocket science to show that Goodwin's conduct was unethical. In fact, the business scandals we hear so much about may give the false impression that it is normally easy to recognize the right decision. We hear about these scandals precisely because they make a sensational story of egregious wrongdoing. Many real-life decisions are murky and difficult to sort out even when one has the best of intentions. In the Interspeed case, for example, there are several hypothetical scenarios in which the right decisions would not be so clear:
   a. Interspeed would be forced into bankruptcy if it didn't show additional revenue in the current period, but it has very good prospects for the future.
   b. In addition to the previous scenario, Interspeed makes products that save lives.
   c. There is a signed contract in which the third party agrees to buy the goods at the beginning of the new year.
   d. Interspeed offers Solunet a percentage of the final sales for buying the product before the end of the year and passing it on to the other customer at the beginning of the new year.
      Your task is to analyze the case under each of these scenarios.
      *Hints.* For Scenario (a), look at the conditions under which income smoothing can be ethical in the analysis of Case 6.1. Scenario (b) asks in effect whether the end justifies the means, an issue discussed in Chapter 2. You must test the generalizability of fudging numbers when saving lives is part of the rationale (i.e., part of the scope). Note that saving lives is part of the scope only if Interspeed would avoid fudging numbers if its existence as a company were at stake, but lives were not. You may assume that the scheme in Scenario (d) is consistent with GAAP.
3. *Celebrity endorsement.*[21] L&L Advertising just signed a contract with movie star Lance Willard for celebrity endorsements of Bud's Best bacon. The president of the firm assigns the account to Annie, who soon learns the awkward fact that Lance has just become a vegetarian. The president assures her that all legal requirements for the endorsement are satisfied, but Annie is uneasy and consults the American Advertising Federation's *Advertising Ethics and Principles.* It states that "advertising containing testimonials shall be limited to those of competent witnesses who are reflecting a real and honest opinion or experience." When Annie interviews Lance, he assures her that Bud's Best has been his favorite brand of bacon since he was a kid. However, he learned during a recent medical checkup that his cholesterol is dangerously high, and his doctor advised him to avoid such high-cholesterol foods as bacon and eggs.

He decided to avoid all meat, for good measure. Annie diplomatically asks Lance if he is comfortable endorsing bacon. Lance responds that his conscience is clean, because he will describe only the taste and quality of the product, which he genuinely believes are tops, and say nothing about whether bacon is healthy. If consumers are going to eat bacon, they may as well eat the best. Besides, many persons can eat a reasonable amount of bacon without adverse health effects. It is up to consumers to decide what kind of diet is right for them. Is it ethical for L&L to use Lance's endorsement? Is it ethical for Lance to give it?

4. *Deterring car theft with Lojack.*[22] Lojack is a hidden radio transmitter device used for retrieving stolen vehicles. Because a potential thief cannot tell whether Lojack has been installed, it is not a deterrent to stealing a particular car. However, statistical analysis shows that the presence of Lojack in many cars deters theft generally. Automobile insurance companies can provide an incentive for car owners to install Lojack by giving a price break to those who do. This benefits the community as well as the insurance companies.

However, an individual insurance company does not have a clear incentive to provide a rate differential. Unless it dominates the market, the reduced premium will reduce its own revenues while having only a small effect on theft—probably not enough to compensate for the revenue loss. Customers with Lojack are more likely to get their car back, and this may result in smaller claims to the company. But this doesn't justify a rate differential large enough to reduce the rate of car theft. Thus in the absence of a dominant player, none of the insurance companies have an incentive to take an action that would be mutually beneficial if they all took it. Do insurance companies have an obligation to provide a rate differential when such a pricing scheme, generally adopted, would make everyone better off?

*Hints.* Don't just say, "This is the government's responsibility." Such a claim requires argument, and even if it is true, private insurers may be obligated to take on the responsibility if the government doesn't act. Also, recall that the utilitarian test doesn't ask how much utility is created if all companies provide a rate differential, but how much is created if one company (the decision maker) does so.

5. *The MasterDept lockbox problem.*[23] MasterDebt, a credit card company, receives thousands of payment checks from cardholders every month. The company wants to exploit float so as to earn as much as possible in interest and fees. Float is the time lapse between the deposit of a payment check and crediting the amount to MasterDept. Cardholders pay interest on any outstanding balance, and MasterDebt wants to maximize float to collect more interest from them, and perhaps late fees as well.

The plan is to maximize float by establishing lockboxes in several cities. Cardholders in each region will be instructed to send their checks to a certain lockbox, perhaps a distant one to maximize float. The company is considering six cities as possible lockbox locations, each of which carries a certain annual fixed cost. The company asked its technical staff to select lockbox locations and assignments that maximize the difference between interest earned from float and the cost of the lockboxes. The solution is far from obvious, but the lockbox problem can be formulated as an uncapacitated facility location problem, a well-known mathematical model used in operations research. Solution of the problem reveals that the location of the lockboxes makes a substantial difference in net benefit to the company.

Lockbox location problems have been solved for many years but raise ethical issues. The interest gained by MasterDebt is interest lost by its customers. One can ask whether MasterDebt has the right to collect this interest at the customer's expense. But this is only an assertion, not an argument. Even if we accept it, we must decide how much delay is artificial. Two days? Three days? There are also legal issues involved, partly due to new credit card regulations recently enacted in the United States.[24] We take it for granted that credit card companies should abide by regulations. Let's focus here on what would be their ethical obligations without specific laws governing the float period. Your task: arrive at an ethical lockbox location and assignment policy.

*Hint.* Delay in processing checks incurs social costs because it introduces uncertainty, makes it more difficult for people to manage cash flow, and may result in less-than-optimal use of their funds. The interest earned by the credit card company due to delay may be a rough indication of these social costs, which can be balanced against the cost of locating lockboxes close to customers. Utility might be roughly maximized by modifying the facility location model so that it minimizes the sum of the interest cost to consumers and the cost of the lockboxes. You should also apply the generalization principle and virtue ethics (think about why we have financial services professionals).

6. *Insider trading.*[25] On November 17, 2008, the SEC filed charges against Mark Cuban for insider trading. The SEC complaint said that Momma.com, an Internet search engine firm, gave Cuban advance notice of a stock offering at below-market price, on the condition that he would keep this information confidential. Cuban already held a good deal of stock in the company and predicted that the new offering would bring down the market price. As a result, he sold all of his stock. The market price in fact fell the day after the offering was announced to the public. Cuban's early sale allowed him to avoid losses of $750,000. An SEC official stated, "Mamma.com entrusted Mr. Cuban with nonpublic information after he promised to keep the information confidential. Less than four hours later, Mr. Cuban betrayed that trust by placing an order to sell all his shares. It is fundamentally unfair for someone to use access to nonpublic information to improperly gain an edge on the market."

Mark Cuban (allegedly) broke the insider trading law, which is unethical because breaking the law is normally ungeneralizable. But is there anything inherently wrong with insider trading? Would it be ethical if it were legal?

*Hints.* Several arguments, summarized below, have been advanced against insider trading. Do valid applications of the conditions for rational choice underlie any of these arguments?

- It reduces utility. If the trade affects the stock price, a major stockholder can dump his holdings just before bad news is released to the public. This could depress the stock price even more and harm the company. Yet some economists argue that insider trades make everyone better off in the long run because the market has more and earlier information about the company, which leads to more rational investment. If an insider trade has no effect on the stock price, then the trade benefits the trader and presumably hurts no one. (Remember that the utilitarian test is not whether a general practice of insider trading maximizes utility, but whether a particular investor's trade does so.)

- It results in an "unlevel playing field" or, to quote the SEC official, is "fundamentally unfair." Should we treat investment as a competition or sports event that has to be "fair" in some sense? Some argue that if inside trading were standard practice, fewer ordinary investors would buy stocks, because insiders would reap a greater share of the rewards of investing, and less capital would be raised. (Note that the generalization test doesn't ask whether the market would be less efficient, but whether one can rationally believe that inside traders would still be able to achieve their purpose of making more money.)

- It is misappropriation of company information, which is shareholder property, and is therefore essentially theft. Can information about company plans be viewed as property?

- It violates fiduciary duty when the insider is a company officer, because insider trading can harm the company more than it benefits the trader. This doesn't apply to Mark Cuban, but is it a valid argument for company officers?

- It redistributes wealth unjustly because it benefits wealthy inside traders at the expense of small investors.

7. *Consulting for Carnegie Foods.*[26] The Pet Food Division of Carnegie Foods operates the world's second largest pet food cannery at Allentown, Pennsylvania. It ships to five regional distribution centers, which serve such customers as Wal-Mart (40% of its business), BJs, Target, Costco, and others. Despite inventory levels that are substantially higher than the industry average, the company has experienced difficulty maintaining the service levels its customers want. Wal-Mart, in particular, demands a high service level, and it usually gets what it wants due to its market dominance.

Adroit Consulting has been engaged to advise the Pet Food Division on how to manage its supply chain to reduce inventory and improve service. One option that is being pushed internally is to install a two-tier system in which a holding warehouse is placed between the cannery and the distribution centers. Adroit must evaluate this proposal as part of its recommendations. In the meantime, Carnegie Foods has authorized its chief information officer (CIO) to acquire Advanced Planning and Scheduling (APS) software to manage its supply chain. Due to limited resources, the company will not implement APS and Adroit's recommendations simultaneously, and Adroit must advise which to do first.

The case raises at least two ethical issues:

- Should Adroit advise Carnegie to use APS, perhaps at the cost of losing a customer? Supply chain systems like APS are well developed; it is very possible that once Carnegie implements APS, it will have no further need for Adroit's supply chain recommendations.
- Is it ethical to provide Wal-Mart better service than other clients simply because Wal-Mart has the clout to demand it—even though Wal-Mart is paying the same price as the others, or even less?

8. *Writers' strike.*[27] On November 5, 2007, the Writers Guild of America, representing 12,000 writers, struck the Alliance of Motion Picture and Television Producers. A key issue in the strike was the writers' demand for residuals from distribution of their work in "new media"—Internet downloads, Internet Protocol TV (IPTV), streaming video, smart phones, and on-demand cable/satellite programming. The Writers Guild asked for 2.5% of gross income from new media. Writers are normally paid a percentage of future revenues, but excluding those from new media. Is it ethical for a recording studio to keep making money on their work without compensating them?

   *Hints.* It is not enough simply to say that fair compensation is whatever the market dictates. Any such claim should be defended by appeal to the conditions of rational choice. The outcome may depend on some factual issues. To deal with this, analyze the case under the four scenarios in Table 6.2, where the propositions (a) and (b) are:

   **a.** There is reason to believe that paying writers the 2.5% would create more overall utility, because they are currently underpaid and spend much of their time making ends meet by other means.
   **b.** There is reason to believe that the movie/television industry as a whole would not be profitable enough to attract investors if all executives paid writers the 2.5%.

9. *Retrocession.*[28] A large private bank employs relationship managers (RMs) who work with high net worth individuals. The RMs help their clients to manage their substantial wealth, avoid taxes, and so forth. When the clients invest in certain funds, the fund owners remit retrocession payments to the bank as a reward. Consequently, the bank provides its RMs a financial incentive to recommend funds that provide retrocession. In theory, this need not create a conflict of interest for the RMs, because it could incentivize them to recommend a fund with retrocession only when there is a choice among equally attractive investments. It is widely suspected, however, that some RMs bias their recommendations to favor investments that yield them a higher commission. Is it ethical for the bank to provide this kind of incentive?

10. *Tax avoidance.* The private bank mentioned in the previous exercise has a number of European clients for whom it provides substantial tax savings. By exploiting loopholes in complex tax laws, the bank allows some of its wealthy clients to avoid the high tax rates prevalent in their home countries. In some cases, clients pay only a small fraction of the tax they would otherwise owe. Yet these clients achieved their success due, in part, to services provided by their home country. They benefited from an excellent state-funded education and from a stable and productive economy that is highly subsidized and regulated by the state. Is it ethical for the bank to provide this kind of advice?

    *Hint.* First analyze the taxpayer's obligation, and then address the bank's dilemma. Keep in mind that a private bank that fails to provide competitive tax advice is at a severe disadvantage for attracting clients.

| TABLE 6.2 | Four factual scenarios for analyzing the writer's strike dilemma in Exercise 8 | |
|---|---|---|
|  | **(b) is false** | **(b) is true** |
| *(a) is true* |  |  |
| *(a) is false* |  |  |

11. *The Empire Globe Corporation.*[29] Susan Bond is Corporate Economist at Empire Globe Corporation, a chemicals company. CEO John Treadstone created the position so that he could have someone to help him with economic analysis of market trends and company proposals. Bond was attracted to the company by Treadstone's professed philosophy of creating a partnership with stakeholders. He created a "Partnership Conduct Team," consisting of four experienced managers, to develop ethical guidelines that exceed legal requirements and monitor compliance with them. Ten years ago, Treadstone located a processing plant in economically depressed Feldport, Oklahoma, against the advice of his staff, because he believed the company could create an effective partnership with the local players. In fact, they were so eager to attract jobs that the bank offered financing at discounted rates, the town council granted a five-year exemption from real estate taxes, the union (reluctantly) negotiated a no-strike clause, and the power company agreed to a low rate.

    The Feldport plant has recently become an issue, however. As the special concessions expired, profit margins at the plant began to shrink. Treadstone set out to obtain similar concessions for the next few years. He indicated that if the company could not obtain adequate return on its capital investment, it would be obliged to relocate. The company managed to obtain most of what it wanted. The town agreed to a partial tax concession, the union ceded a cap on wages and reinstated the no-strike clause, and the bank provided further financing at below-market rates. However, Empire has not yet obtained the 4.25 cents per kwh rate it wants from the power company. To address this, Treadstone scheduled a negotiation session with the power company, involving himself, Bond, and Jim Doran, the VP for finance.

    It is the day before the session. Bond is already concerned that the company is demanding excessive concessions from the community, but her discomfort grows when she receives a late-afternoon message from Treadstone. It states that he and Doran won't be present for the meeting, due to a commitment in Washington, DC, and that she is on her own. Furthermore, there's a change in strategy. She must obtain a rate of 3.80 cents per kwh.

    The next morning, Bond cancels the meeting and contacts Ted Bates in the finance department to ask for data that might justify demanding a lower rate. Ted lets slip in the conversation that Empire has just landed a lucrative contract with the Defense Department that calls for a 25% increase in production at Feldport. She realizes that this was the agenda for the Washington meeting and that the threat to relocate is a bluff. She first tries to reach Doran, head of the negotiating team, but he finds himself too busy to talk about the issue. She finally calls Treadstone, who acknowledges the Defense contract when Bond brings it up. Bond asks him about his commitment to partnership, whereupon Treadstone responds that the low rate is necessary to justify his bid to Defense, and the added production will mean more jobs in Feldport. Besides, there is nothing wrong with making a profit, and they have obligations to their stockholders. Bond asks what happens if she is unable to get the 3.80 cents per kwh rate. Treadstone responds, "Susan, negotiating means getting agreements. Anything else on your mind?"

    *Hints.* The negotiation principles discussed in Case 6.3 may be useful. A utilitarian analysis can also be central to this case.

12. *Opt in or opt out.*[30] Countries typically use an opt-in or opt-out approach to organ donation. Opt-in countries give people an opportunity to sign a donor card to grant permission to us their organs. Opt-out countries assume that people give permission unless they fill out a form or make a phone call to revoke consent. Johnson and Goldstein[31] report that organ donor consent is much higher in opt-out countries. If permission to donate is the default, people tend to let it stand. They are much more reluctant to give permission by overriding a default. Table 6.3 shows the rates for European countries. (The Netherlands' relatively high opt-in rate is due to an aggressive public campaign.) In the United States, an opt-in country, 85% of people "approve" of organ donation but only 28% grant permission. The article states that more than 45,000 people in the United States died in 1995 while awaiting a donor organ. It suggests that many lives could be saved by switching to an opt-out policy.

    Because opting out requires some effort in Europe, one may ask whether the inconvenience of opting out explains the low rates. Johnson and Goldstein conducted an online survey of 161 U.S. respondents, who were asked to assume that they had just moved to a new state. Question 1 asked them

| TABLE 6.3 | Effective consent rates (percent) for organ donation, by country | | |
|---|---|---|---|
| **Opt-In Countries** | **%** | **Opt-Out Countries** | **%** |
| The Netherlands | 27.5 | Austria | 99.98 |
| United Kingdom | 17.2 | Hungary | 99.97 |
| Germany | 12 | France | 99.91 |
| Denmark | 4.25 | Portugal | 99.64 |
| — | — | Poland | 99.5 |
| — | — | Belgium | 98 |
| — | — | Sweden | 85.9 |

*Source*: Based on Eric J. Johnson and Daniel Goldstein, "Do defaults save lives?" *Science*, 302, November 21, 2003, pp. 1338–1339.

if they would opt in to organ donation if given the opportunity. Question 2 asked if they would opt out. Question 3 asked how they would respond if required to choose whether to donate (with no default). The results (Table 6.4) show that only half as many people donate when required to opt in. Defaults therefore remain a key factor even when no effort is involved.

Is it ethical to use an opt-out system to save lives? Or is it dishonest? A rational agent would presumably make the same choice regardless of the default. The low opt-out rate suggests that an opt-out system plays on psychological factors that distort the agent's true intent. There are substantial opt-in/opt-out differences for online privacy,[32] selection of insurance coverage,[33] and the level of pension savings.[34]

*Hints.* There are several possible explanations for why people opt out, such as:

1. It is too much trouble to opt out.
2. People don't want to think about the choice because of its emotional content.
3. People overlook the matter, perhaps because it is in "fine print," they are busy, or some other reason. Analyze the issue under each scenario.

13. *Preserving a culture.*[35] Bob Littman is owner of a series of galleries and a major client of Artifacts, an importer of ethnic arts. While having lunch with Mary, a manager at Artifacts, he is introduced to Len. A buyer for Artifacts, Len has traveled widely in South America in search of native artwork. One of his major sources is the Amazonia[36] people, whom he has gotten to know quite well, even learning their language. Bob is very interested in Amazonia basketry and indicates that he would like to place a series of large orders, provided the Amazonia will make certain changes in the patterns and colors of their baskets to suit the tastes of his customers. A deal of this magnitude would be highly profitable both for Artifacts and the Amazonia. Mary is enthusiastic about the idea. She proposes that Len return to South America and convince the Amazonia to modify their designs, which should be a minor matter given their obvious skills. Len, however, was an anthropology major in college and understands that the Amazonia basket designs are not just pleasing patterns. Symbolism plays a central and powerful role in

| TABLE 6.4 | Consent rates for organ donation as measured by an online survey |
|---|---|
| Opt-in default | 42% |
| Opt-out default | 82% |
| Neutral | 79% |

*Source*: Based on Eric J. Johnson and Daniel Goldstein, "Do defaults save lives?" *Science*, 302, November 21, 2003, pp. 1338–1339.

many traditional cultures. The design elements that displease Bob contain symbols that denote important events in the group's long history. Even if the Amazonia agree to change their designs, he fears that they may not appreciate the risk of losing their symbolic tradition and the long-term impact on their culture. To make matters worse, meeting the production quotas would require that both men and women work on the baskets. Basket weaving is an integral part of a woman's role in Amazonia culture and never undertaken by men. The honor of preserving and celebrating the history of their people inspires women to spend a lifetime mastering the intricate designs. If Len explains all this to Mary, should she ask him to take this assignment? If she does, how should Len deal with the request?

*Hint.* A principle stated at the beginning of the next chapter may be helpful in analyzing this case.

## Notes

1. Based on SEC Litigation Release 20333, *SEC v. Nortel Networks Corporation and Nortel Networks Limited*, October 15, 2007; E. Mathieu and S. Freeman, "Three ex-Nortel executives charged," *Toronto Star*, June 19, 2008; and other news reports. My thanks to Caroline Levine for suggesting this case.

2. Based on *The Ford-Firestone Case*, by Michael Pinedo, Sridhar Seshadri, and Eitan Zemel, Stern School of Business, 2001. My thanks to Alan Scheller-Wolf for suggesting this case.

3. Alan B. Krueger and Alexandre Mas, "Strikes, scabs and tread separations: Labor strife and the production of defective Bridgestone/Firestone tires," *Journal of Political Economy*, 112(2), 2004, pp. 253–289.

4. Although the strike also affected the Oklahoma City plant, it largely escaped the quality problems of the Decatur plant. It would be interesting to look at whether and how management practices differed there.

5. Based on the case study *Bullard Houses*, by Ron Karp, David Gold, and Mox Tan, Program on Negotiation at Harvard University, 2004. My thanks to Don Moore for suggesting this case.

6. Years ago, while working for a national laboratory, I was asked to present a report at the Department of Energy in Washington, D.C. Some lobbyists presented the industry side at the same meeting. When I talked informally with them afterward, they told me that they didn't believe a word of what they said in the meeting room. They said what they were paid to say. They apparently felt an obligation to level with me as a human being, but not with the organization I represented.

7. Based on the case study, *Marketing Antidepressants: Prozac and Paxil*, Harvard Case 9-502-055, by Y. Moon and K. Herman, 2002. My thanks to Joachim Vosgerau for suggesting this case.

8. There may be a utilitarian case against *legalizing* direct-to-consumer marketing of drugs, which is a different issue. It is possible that when direct-to-consumer marketing is legal, companies inevitably abuse the privilege by making ads that mislead. It may also be impractical to regulate the content of the ads well enough to prevent abuse. A utilitarian test may therefore require laws against direct-to-consumer marketing, unless such laws are unethical on other grounds.

9. One can "manipulate" without deception, as when one seduces a lover, and the lover knows what is going on. But this kind of "manipulation" is perfectly OK!

10. Based on various news reports. My thanks to Bryan Routledge for suggesting this case.

11. In an interview with Maria Bartiromo of CNBC on March 13, 2007.

12. Ignoring the loan contract altogether is clearly ungeneralizable. Contracts could not exist if people ignored them whenever its suits their purpose. But the proposal here is to work out a modification of the contract. The borrower is still going to pay off the mortgage, but in smaller installments.

13. Countrywide could avoid foreclosure by relaxing the terms *more* that everyone else does, but this is clearly ungeneralizable. It is impossible for all lenders to relax terms more than all other lenders.

14. Compensation may in fact be required by law for many of the subprime loans, and many lawsuits have been filed. But I won't try to resolve the legal issue.

15. Based on the film *Super Size Me*, written and directed by Morgan Spurlock, Kathbur Pictures, 2004. My thanks to Anita Woolley for suggesting this case.

16. Based on the case study, *Block 16: Conoco's "Green" Oil Strategy*, by Susan E. A. Hall and Malcolm S. Salter, Harvard Case 9-394-001 (1993). My thanks to Lester Lave for suggesting this case.

17. Due to opposition of indigenous and environmental groups, Conoco later sold its Block 16 rights to Maxus

Corporation, a relatively small U.S operation. Maxus was then eventually bought out by YPF (Argentina). But ConocoPhillips was back in Ecuador in 2006 when it bought Burlington Resources. It has drilling rights in two blocks and in many respects faces again the issues raised in this case. Burlington had not been able to move forward with drilling due to local and international opposition.

18. Douglas Lockwood, *I, the Aboriginal.* Sydney, Lansdowne Publishing, 2000.
19. Based on the case study *Hank Kolb, Director, Quality Assurance*, by Frank S. Leonard, Harvard Case 9-681-083, 1981. My thanks to Alan Scheller-Wolf for suggesting this case.
20. Based on news reports and SEC Litigation Release 20126, *Securities and Exchange Commission v. Arthur A. Goodwin*, May 23, 2007. My thanks to Caroline Levine for suggesting this case and the four hypothetical scenarios described here.
21. Based on the Arthur Andersen mini-case *The Nonuser Celebrity Endorser* by Geoffrey P. Lantos.
22. Based on Ian Ayres and Steven D. Levitt, "Measuring positive externalities from unobservable victim precaution: An empirical analysis of Lojack," *Quarterly Journal of Economics*, 113, February 1998, pp. 43–77. My thanks to Dennis Epple for suggesting this case.
23. Based on Case 6.3 in Cliff T. Ragsdale, *Spreadsheet Modeling and Decision Analysis*, 5th ed., Thomson, 2007, pp. 293–294. My thanks to François Margot for suggesting this case.
24. *Credit Card Accountability, Responsibility, and Disclosure Act* (Credit CARD Act) of 2009.
25. Based on U.S. Securities and Exchange Commission press release, *SEC Files Insider Trading Charges against Mark Cuban*, November 17, 2008. My thanks to Bryan Routledge for suggesting this case.
26. Based on the case study, *Production and Inventory Strategy: Developing a Production and Inventory Plan for Carnegie Foods*, developed for classroom use by Deloitte Consulting, 2008. Carnegie Foods is a fictitious name. My thanks to Sunder Kekre for suggesting this case.
27. My thanks to Bryan Routledge for suggesting this case.
28. Based on case studies provided by executive workshop participants.
29. Based on the Arthur Andersen case study *The Empire Globe Corporation* by Clarence Walton and Edwin M. Epstein.
30. My thanks to Joachim Vosgerau for suggesting this case.
31. Eric J. Johnson and Daniel Goldstein, "Do defaults save lives?" *Science*, 302, November 21, 2003, pp. 1338–1339.
32. S. Bellman, E. J. Johnson, and G. L. Lohse, "On site: to opt-in or opt-out? It depends on the question," *Communications of the ACM*, 44(2), February 2001, pp. 25–27. E. J. Johnson, S. Bellman, and G. L. Lohse, "Defaults, framing and privacy: Why opting in-opting out?" *Marketing Letters*, 13(1), February 2002, pp. 5–15.
33. E. J. Johnson, J. Hershey, J. Meszaros, and H. Kunreuther, "Framing, probability, distortions, and insurance decisions," *Journal of Risk Uncertainty*, 7(1), 1993, pp. 35–51.
34. B. C. Madrian and D. Shea, "The power of suggestion: Inertia in 401(k) participation and savings behavior," *Quarterly Journal of Economics*, 116(4), 2001, pp. 1149–1187.
35. Based on the Arthur Andersen mini-case *Societal Impacts of Marketing* by Judy Cohen.
36. A fictitious group.

# Chapter 7

# Cross-Cultural Ethics

U p to this point, our analysis has been grounded in the Western ethical tradition. In this final chapter, we broaden our perspective by briefly examining other ethical systems. The purpose is twofold. One is to alert you to the fact that ethical norms can be very different around the world. A single chapter can scarcely provide an adequate treatment of world ethical cultures, but perhaps an initial exposure to their variety will inspire you to learn more before your next assignment abroad. A second purpose is to throw more light on the Western tradition by contrasting it with other systems. A useful way to understand who you are is to learn who you are not.

It is essential to avoid two mistakes from the outset. One is the prevalent idea that the great ethical systems are at root very similar, and they differ only in details that reflect differences in regional environments. This is simply untrue. Normative systems around the world are based on radically different presuppositions, ultimately on different ontological conceptions of human nature. The implications for everyday life are sometimes similar, because all the systems must enable human beings to live together, but they can be very different as well. There are many ways to structure a society, and they are reflected in different ethical norms.

A second and related mistake is that some cultures are simply less ethical than others, as witnessed by high levels of corruption and social dysfunction. The reality is more complicated. All cultures suffer from corruption, but the corruption takes different forms. Corruption is activity that corrupts: It tends to undermine the cultural system in which it occurs. Because different cultures have different ways of getting things done, different kinds of activity corrupt them. Nepotism and cronyism, for example, tend to be corrupting in Western cultures but can, in the right circumstances, represent high moral virtue in other cultures. What appears to be corruption may be entirely functional.

Another complication is that all cultures have weak points that lead them to break down in different ways. Bribery tends to be more prevalent in some non-Western cultures, but cheating poses an equally grave risk to Western cultures. Westerners tend to notice the bribery abroad and to forget about the serious threat of cheating at home.

Finally, cultures may fall into dysfunction due to such disruptions as famine, economic hardship, military defeat, and external domination. It is easy to think of many historical cases in which both Western and non-Western cultures have abandoned their ethical norms when under stress.

We focus here on the phenomenon of corruption because it provides a useful introduction to cross-cultural ethics. Not only does it illustrate the difference among cultural systems but is also a very practical issue that confronts many business people. The chapter is organized around a series of case studies that illustrate various kinds of corruption.[1] There are no exercises, because the chapter provides insufficient background to build skills in cross-cultural decision making. The material here is intended only as a starting point.

## CROSS-CULTURAL DECISIONS

Understanding another normative system is one thing, but how do we make ethical decisions when another system is different than our own? Should we stick to our principles, or do as the Romans do?

Actually, each culture has its own ethical resources for cross-cultural interaction. Peoples have related to each other, and done business with each other, since prehistoric times. Western cultures present a peculiar problem in this respect, because they tend to be universalizing cultures. For reasons we will discuss shortly, Westerners tend to believe that there can be only one rational approach to life and, in particular, only one legitimate ethical system. This is perhaps why Westerners so readily find commonality across the world's ethical norms. Nonetheless, even Western ethics has a principle that can help us navigate cross-cultural encounters.

That principle is Corollary 1 of the generalization test: An action is unethical if its general adoption would undermine a practice it presupposes. It can be paraphrased for cross-cultural situations as follows:

- An action is unethical if its general adoption in the host culture would undermine a practice it presupposes.

We will use this principle as a basis for analyzing case studies. It is by no means a complete guide, but it can take us a long way and help us to avoid many blunders that are often made in cross-cultural encounters.

## RELATIONSHIPS VS. RULES

A first step toward understanding cultural difference is to distinguish *rule-based* cultures from *relationship-based* cultures. Whereas Western cultures are primarily rule based, most of the world's cultures are relationship based. Westerners tend to trust the system, while people elsewhere trust their friends and family. Westerners organize their business around contracts or agreements that are enforced by a legal system. Other cultures may organize their business around human relationships that are cemented by personal honor, filial duty, friendship, or long-term mutual obligation.

Rule-based cultures are universalizing because this is necessary to make the system work. Westerners see themselves as autonomous individuals, none of whom has inherent authority over others. Rulers and bosses inherit authority from rules or contracts that specify their powers and how they are selected for office. Westerners must therefore respect the rules for their own sake. Rules command this kind of obedience only when they are seen as inherently logical and reasonable. Because logic is universal, legitimate rules are viewed as universally valid. For example, Westerners expect everyone to see the internal logic of a laissez-faire market system, or of democratic politics based on elections and majority rule.

Westerners are often taught to feel guilty when they violate rules whose internal logic they recognize. Western societies may therefore rely heavily on guilt feelings, along with fear of punishment if caught, to encourage good behavior. Personal supervision tends to be relatively light. Transparency is important, because it helps to verify that everyone is going by the book.

Relationship-based cultures have rules, but the rules are legitimized and enforced in a different way. People tend to respect authority figures rather than rules for their own sake. Rules obtain their legitimacy from the authority figures who issue them. Enforcement, both in the family and at the workplace, tends to take the form of constant personal supervision. Bad behavior can result in shame or loss of face, as opposed to guilt.

Naturally, legal systems and other rule-based mechanisms may operate in a relationship-based culture, especially when there is Western influence. Conversely, personal connections are important in Western cultures. Yet in either case, one can distinguish the main system from auxiliary mechanisms.

Equipped with the broad distinction between rule-based and relationship-based cultures, we can begin to investigate why corruption can take different forms in Western and non-Western countries.

## Cronyism and the Purchasing Agent

Purchasing agents in a Western company are expected to award contracts based on the quality of bids and transparently available financial information about the bidders. An agent who favors personal friends is viewed as corrupt, because cronyism creates a conflict of interest. A choice that is good for the agent and his or her cronies may not be good for the company.

In much of the world, however, cronyism is a foundation for trust. A purchasing agent does business with friends because friends can be trusted. It is assumed that cronies will follow through on the deal, not because they fear a lawsuit, but because they don't wish to sacrifice a valuable relationship in an economy where relationships are the key to business. In such a system, it is in the *company's* interest for the agent to do business with friends.

Responsible cronyism may therefore present no conflict of interest. Far from being a form of corruption, it may be essential to good business. Cronyism becomes irresponsible when the agent does business with friends simply because they are friends and not because they are trustworthy business partners. Rule-based behavior can likewise be irresponsible, as when the agent doesn't exercise due diligence in comparing bids and researching the vendors.

## Inappropriate Lawsuits

Lawsuits are routine and necessary in the West, which relies on rules and individual responsibility. In Japan, however, they can be corrupting. Japan is a strongly relationship-based culture in which interpersonal relations are based on maintaining harmony. Harmony is preserved by elaborate courtesies, humility, deference to superiors, and avoidance of confrontation. After a 1985 Japan Air Lines crash, CEO Yasumoto Tagaki traveled the country to apologize personally to families of the victims and offered educational benefits to children who lost their parents. He subsequently resigned.[2] The apology and resignation don't indicate personal guilt as in the West, and the benefits were not the result of a lawsuit. In fact, Boeing repairs were apparently at fault, not the airline. The intent was to make amends. Another dramatic illustration of this principle was provided when Shohei Nozawa made a tearful apology to employees and stockholders shortly after Yamaichi Securities declared bankruptcy in 1997. Nozawa was not admitting guilt and in fact had just assumed his position as CEO in order to clean up a mess left by others. His aim was to restore harmony among the stakeholders.

Even Western-style negotiation can disrupt harmony in Confucian cultures. Westerners tend to organize their affairs around agreements, deals, or contracts, relying on a concept of covenant that traces back to the ancient Middle East. These agreements are worked out in negotiation, for example, when labor and management sit across the table from each other. This practice is functional and constructive, so long as it proceeds according to rules of fair play and good faith.

Confucian cultures, by contrast, are based primarily on loyalty and obligation to friends, family, or superiors rather than on a system of rules. There is a traditional preference for building relationships rather than making deals. Bargaining across the table tends to be regarded as confrontation rather than negotiation, even when it is strictly regulated by protocol, as in Japan. Bargaining is confrontational in street markets precisely because the parties typically don't have a working relationship. This kind of bargaining is acceptable when long-term collaboration is not required. But when undertaking long-term projects, it is best to develop harmony and trust among the parties rather than rely on Western-style negotiation.

### Bribery

Bribery is corrupting in the West because it induces people to depart from the rules. If bribes become common enough, people in general may lose faith in the system and flout the rules routinely. Bribery is normally corrupting in relationship-based cultures as well, but for a different reason: It shortcuts the building of stable relationships on which society relies. A bribe "buys" a relationship only until the next bribe is required.

Bribery tends to be more prevalent in relationship-based cultures, because a genuine relationship requires time and effort to build, and there is a temptation to take shortcuts. There can also be a fine line between legitimate relationships and quid pro quo bribery, which makes it easier to slip from one to the other.

Rule-based systems, on the other hand, are particularly vulnerable to cheating, because behavior is much less likely to be regulated by direct personal supervision. Minimal supervision imposes less social and economic overhead, but it also carries risks. Rule-based institutions rely largely on voluntary good behavior, and when a critical mass of people fall short, stability is threatened. The financial crisis of 2008–2009 provides an excellent example, because irresponsible behavior on the part of relatively few lightly supervised actors precipitated a worldwide credit freeze in a Western-oriented financial system.

By contrast, business in relationship-based cultures is organized around relationships with families, friends, and bosses, who constantly monitor behavior. This kind of supervision carries a higher social cost, and it takes longer to get things done, but a distributed system of personal relationships can be more stable.

## CASE 7.1

## Kickbacks in Taiwan

### SYNOPSIS[3]

Don, a manager for a U.S.-based manufacturer, was assigned to his company's Taiwan branch. Shortly after his assignment, he met with a team representing a potential local supplier. After the team departed, he noticed that one of them had left behind a briefcase. While looking for the owner's name, he found the valise to be full of cash. He immediately realized that the cash was intended as a kickback, or a bribe to induce him to source from this particular firm. He decided to refuse it, partly due to a clearly articulated company policy against receiving such payments. He dispatched a trusted subordinate to return the briefcase to the owner. He then sent a vaguely worded message to the owner's boss stating that he was

returning lost property. The owner undoubtedly got the cash from his boss, and Don didn't want him to keep it and leave his boss with the impression that the money had been delivered. The boss was actually relieved that, in this case at least, no kickback was expected.

### ANALYSIS

China and Taiwan rely on the stability provided by long-term relationships of mutual obligation known as *guānxì* (Mandarin Chinese for "connection"). *Guānxì* comes into play when business requires trust relationships between people who are not part of the same family or organization. The relationship may begin with a gift, which might be reciprocated with a fine dinner. The process continues, until eventually one party is securing customers for the other, or the second is finding jobs for relatives of the first. These favors are neither quid pro quo nor bribes. If they were quid pro quo, the relationship would evaporate as soon as one party failed to reciprocate. Yet dishonesty or failure to follow through on a promise can endanger the relationship, and both parties therefore have reason to trust the other in business dealings. Neither party wants to risk losing valuable *guānxì* in which he or she has invested over the years.

Kickbacks are common in Taiwan but are corrupting nonetheless. They are attempts to create a relationship without the hard work of building *guānxì*. If all business relationships outside a common family or organization were based on such payments, there would be too little predictability to support a successful economy. The economic system on which Don relies to do business in Taiwan would be undermined. Accepting the kickback would therefore violate the generalization principle articulated above.

On the other hand, cronyism can be functional in this context. It may not be a corrupt act for Don to award the contract to a trusted friend with whom he had done business for years, even if that person's bid is not the lowest. This could be in the company's interest, because personal trust in the vendor may be well worth the premium the company must pay. Company policy may not recognize this fact, of course, and Don would have to take this into account. ▪

---

## CASE 7.2

# Bribery in India

## SYNOPSIS

The Indian economy in 1992 was on the threshold of becoming the information-age powerhouse it is today. India's Congress party had just introduced sweeping market reforms, under the leadership of Prime Minister P. V. Narasimha Rao and his finance minister Manmohan Singh (later to become Prime Minister). One firm that foresaw India's potential was Enron, which predicted that reliable electric power would play a central role in the country's new information economy. The company joined with Bechtel and General Electric to finance a gigantic power plant at Dabhol, in Maharashtra State. It was to be India's largest-ever private foreign investment.

However, the cost of generating power at the plant was projected to be substantially greater than the prevailing rate, partly because it would be fueled by liquefied natural gas from Qatar. Despite this liability, the Indian government guaranteed Enron a very generous return on investment. There were suggestions, particularly from the opposition Bharatiya Janata Party (BJP), that bribery was involved.[4] This and other accusations of corruption in the Congress Party, along with a Hindu nationalist uprising, thrust the BJP into power in 1998. Meanwhile, prominent journalist Raghu Dhar claimed that Enron tried to bribe him to withdraw his opposition to the Dabhol plant.[5] Public opinion turned against the project, and protestors descended on the construction site.

The BJP eventually backed off from the Enron deal when it took power, despite appeals from U.S. Vice President Dick Cheney and Secretary of State Colin Powell to honor the commitment. A small portion of the plant finally began operating in 1999, but only in fits and starts, and most of the plant sits idle to this day.

## ANALYSIS

Bribery is a fact of life in India, and one could take the attitude that one should "do as the Romans do." Yet the previous case study shows that common practice is not a reliable indicator of what is corrupting and what is not. The system may operate in spite of prevalent behavior rather than because of it. Conversely, one could infer that bribery is corrupting in such cases from the fact that Indians widely disapprove of it—at least when bribery is understood as high-level influence peddling, as opposed to small "grease" payments. Yet what people say or think about a practice is not the relevant test. The test for corruption is whether the practice tends to undermine the system.

India is a relationship-based culture that relies only to some extent on imported Western institutions. The primary mechanism for getting things done is a highly developed skill for working through social and family networks. The government is parliamentary, but power is often exercised through a remarkably resilient web of personal and family connections. The country can weather widespread riots and communal violence, as occurred after the 1992 destruction of the Babri mosque in Ayodhya, without a serious threat to its stability.

Bribery threatens social stability to the extent that it displaces traditional networking. If Enron had established itself in India by working through connections with influential people, its conduct would have been consistent with the cultural system—even if Westerners (and many Indians) might prefer a transparent approach involving bids and contracts. But bribery is a double liability, because it corrupts India's quasi-Western institutions, particularly the judicial system, as well as its traditional social networking. If Enron executives actually paid bribes, they violated the generalization principle. ▪

## CASE 7.3

# Nepotism in China

### SYNOPSIS[6]

Lee Kam Sheung founded an oyster sauce business in rural Guangdong Province, China, in 1888. By 2005, the family-owned company had become a major food and health products firm, Lee Kum Kee (LKK) Ltd., based in Hong Kong. It operated plants in China, Malaysia, Philippines, and the United States. It sold its products in 80 countries and employed 3,900 workers. Lee's grandson Man Tat was Group Chairman and had appointed his four sons to serve as chairmen and/or CEOs of various divisions.

Lee Man Tat recognized the importance of bringing professional managerial expertise into his company. He sent his sons to college in the United States and then persuaded them (primarily by an appeal to filial duty) to join the company as top managers. By 2005, the board of directors contained two outsiders, in addition to himself and his sons. He planned to add two more outsiders to the board and to recruit high-level managers. He explicitly stated that he sought professional managers who were comfortable with the fact that the firm's top executives were family members.

### ANALYSIS

Some Western managers would be uncomfortable with the obvious nepotism in LKK. Should they be uncomfortable with it? Is it corrupting?

Actually, nepotism can be functional in a Confucian setting. The extended family is historically the primary unit of economic survival in China. It exhibits the discipline and loyalty necessary to scrape out a living in a harsh environment. The parents and grandparents exercise a degree of authority unusual in the West, and everyone puts family before self. This tradition is very much alive today, particularly in Taiwan, Hong Kong, and many overseas Chinese communities, although it is evolving in the large cities.

Westerners associate nepotism with the lazy or incompetent relative on the staff, but it can have advantages in a Confucian setting. A Chinese manager may extract more work from his sons, grandsons, and nephews than from nonfamily members. Relatives may not be the most talented available candidates for the job, but grandfather or uncle knows their strengths and weaknesses intimately and can make the best use of their skills. Nepotism, no less than cronyism, must be used responsibly to benefit the firm as well as the individuals concerned. Lee Man Tat evidently succeeded in this. As a result, there is no obvious reason that Western managers should have ethical reservations about working for LKK.

Chinese have long recognized that nepotism can be problematic in government. The Sui Dynasty introduced civil service exams for the state bureaucracy 14 centuries ago. Today, nepotism is often illegal, or at least officially discouraged, in government agencies and state-owned enterprises. Inappropriate nepotism can therefore be corrupting even in a Confucian context. Nonetheless, family business, and the nepotism that often goes with it, remains a central Chinese institution outside the mainland and is increasingly reasserting itself in the mainland, as nonstate firms proliferate.

LKK also demonstrates that nepotism can adjust itself to global business. Although the family members expect to maintain control, they are aware of possible cultural complications. They intentionally avoid antagonizing outside professionals with the kind of close supervision that is characteristic of relationship-based cultures. ▪

## CASE 7.4

# Accounting Fraud in North America

### SYNOPSIS

Case 6.1, "Nortel and Income Smoothing," illustrates corruption in its most prevalent Western form: cheating. The case describes how executives at Nortel improperly used bill-and-hold transactions as an income smoothing device. Actually, this is only one of their unethical activities. For example, Nortel delivered goods to a minority-owned business Telamon, which sold the goods to customers who were required to source a certain percentage of their supplies from minority- or women-owned businesses. Nortel recognized the revenue from sale of the goods when it delivered them to Telamon. This is permitted by U.S. GAAP, however, only if Telamon accepts the risk of ownership, which it did not, because it routinely returned unsold goods to Nortel.

These and other schemes led the U.S. Securities and Exchange Commission to file civil charges, and some executives eventually paid fines in an out-of-court settlement. The Ontario Securities Commission subsequently pressed fraud charges against three executives, who were arrested in June 2008.[7] Nortel filed for bankruptcy in January 2009. Five months later, it announced its intention to cease business operations and sell off all assets.

## ANALYSIS

Nortel's behavior is corrupting because transparency is a foundation of the system in which the company operates. By and large, North American investors have not developed a tradition of cultivating friends and extended family relationships through which

they can channel investment capital. On the contrary, it is common advice not to get financially involved with friends and families, because of the friction that can result. It is therefore necessary to invest in companies whose managers are essentially strangers. This, in turn, requires some reliable way to obtain information about the firm. Professional accounting practices meet this need by making the firm transparent to investors.

The case illustrates the ease with which rules can be violated in the limited-oversight environment of a rule-based system. These Nortel executives were deterred neither by guilt feelings nor by fear of being caught. In fact, one suspects that they were eventually caught only because they perpetrated sustained and rather egregious violations of accounting standards over a period of three years. ■

## CASE 7.5

# Corruption in Sub-Saharan Africa

### SYNOPSIS[8]

Dr. Mo Ibrahim and Terry Rhodes founded Celtel International, a wireless service provider, in 1998. They recognized that sub-Saharan Africa was a largely untapped market for mobile phone service. In addition, Ibrahim (Sudanese by origin) wanted to contribute to African economic development. He was personally aware of the obstacles of doing business in the region but believed they could be overcome.

Ibrahim and Rhodes resolved to play it clean if at all possible. In some cases, they avoided side payments simply by waiting out customs and other officials who demanded money in exchange for timely approval. On one occasion, they transformed the arrival of their equipment into a public relations event, so that the customs officer could not delay matters without personal embarrassment. On another occasion, they contributed to a school rather than bribe the local chief directly.

However, in Guinea they encountered an impasse.[9] Celtel had purchased a $750,000 operating license from the Guinean government, but there were delays in the steps necessary to implement the license. Finally, Rhodes and colleagues set up a meeting with key government officials who could clear the way. When they arrived at the meeting, however, there was an awkward silence. The Guinean officials looked as though they were expecting something, and when disappointed, the meeting reached a deadlock.

Rhodes learned afterward that a fax had arrived in Celtel's Amsterdam headquarters before the meeting. It listed the officials who would be present. Next to the names were monetary amounts, totaling about $50,000, demanded in exchange for setting up the meeting. Further bribes would be necessary to implement the

license. Due to poor telephone service in Guinea, the headquarters staff could not alert him to the fax.

### ANALYSIS

Much of the bribery that is so common in sub-Saharan Africa can be traced to cultural disruption. It is hard to make generalizations about a region that contains hundreds of cultures and languages, but a common theme across many of them is their traditional village orientation. The coming of colonialism, and later globalization, undermined the role of leaders in village life. Leaders traditionally retained power by judicious redistribution of resources. Their privileges allow them to accumulate wealth, and they in turn endow their subjects with gifts and favors. Anthropologists refer to this as a "big man" institution, first described as such in Melanesia. The big man system may have evolved because a community has greater survival advantage when the chief can rationally redistribute wealth to where it is most needed.

When colonial powers brought Western practices to sub-Saharan Africa, many men left villages to take jobs at commercial farms and mines, while leaders often got government positions in cities. They took with them the practice of obtaining influence through generosity, but they left behind the village context that structured and guided this practice. To oversimplify a complicated story, responsible distribution of wealth to maintain influence degenerated into payment of bribes to buy influence.

Africans with whom I have worked are intensely aware of this dynamic and resent the fact that foreign corporations often acquiesce in paying bribes. They point out that bribery requires a briber as well as a bribee. Bribery is not so much a form of corruption as a particularly visible symptom of a deeper corruption. Paying bribes is nonetheless ungeneralizable to the extent that it contributes to an already corrupted social order.

One way to align one's business with the generalization principle is to mimic the ancient function of generosity. A company can try to distribute resources to where they are most needed without passing them through corrupt channels. This could mean investments in schools and infrastructure, as well as economic development through the funding of microloans. More importantly, foreign investors can establish business operations that add value to the local economy rather than simply extracting resources. ■

---

# CASE 7.6

# Side Payments in the Middle East

## SYNOPSIS[10]

On arrival at a Turkish airport, an MBA student from the United States joined the passport control queue. On reaching the front of the queue, he handed his passport to the official. Rather than stamping the passport, the official put it in a drawer and proceeded to process the next few travelers in the queue. Perplexed, the student asked if there was a problem. The official responded that there was no problem that US$50 would not fix. The student reluctantly pulled out his wallet and handed over the money. At this point, the official returned his passport, but without a stamp, and continued to process the queue. When the student asked whether his passport could be stamped, the official responded that certainly, it could, but this would require another US$50.

## ANALYSIS

Side payments are a fact of life in Turkey. In one survey of a cross-section of the population, about half of the respondents admitted to paying at least one bribe in the previous two years.[11] The payments are despised by those who must pay them, but they are not always corrupting. They need not undermine a cultural mechanism in the way that kickbacks can undermine and displace *guānxì*. The airport payments are not corrupting, because they have little or no effect on whether travelers are properly cleared through passport control (the traveler has little choice but to pay up). Nor does it displace a relationship-oriented practice that would other operate. The traveler's airport payment (but not the official's demand) therefore passes the generalization test.

Many payments in Turkey are less innocuous, however. They span the gamut from traffic fixes to high-level influence peddling. They can distort decision making and the implementation of much-needed policies. Underlying the corruption is the introduction of Western institutions into a relationship-based culture. It is a common phenomenon around the world but a particularly explicit one in Turkey because of Kemal Atatürk's efforts to Westernize the Turkish state he founded after the First World War. Traditional Turkish culture, whose roots extend deep into Asia, is not designed to support a Western-style bureaucracy that relies heavily on unsupervised adherence to rules.

The eastern, relationship-oriented side of Turkish culture remains functional in many contexts. In a typical scenario, the foreign visitor is welcomed with warm hospitality, that being the Turkish tradition. When it surfaces that the visitor is having difficulty with the system, the host asks some old friends to take care of it. This is not corruption but appropriate behavior for a people who for centuries have been bound together by friendship and hospitality rather than adherence to rules and procedure.

## THE MIDDLE EAST AND WASTA

Turkey and other Middle Eastern countries historically invest authority in persons rather than rules. One typically cannot get something done simply by following procedures, although this may be necessary, but must have the support of influential people. Businesspeople working in Arab countries, particularly in the Gulf area, frequently tell of projects in which nothing much happens until the appropriate *sheikh* or authority figure gives the go-ahead, whereupon everything falls into place. This in itself is not corruption, because there are traditional checks and balances on power. Leading families command respect and therefore retain power in part because they have a tradition of exercising power responsibly.

This raises the question as to how one obtains the sponsorship of an authority figure. In traditional Arab culture, the *sheikh* ideally holds a *majlis* (Arabic for "sitting place") to hear petitions and grant favors when warranted. Today, it is often necessary to work through someone who has the ear of an influential person. Such a person is popularly known as a *wasta*, who is an intermediary who petitions an authority figure on behalf of a client. The word can also refer to the influence that the *wasta* offers. *Wasta* is often used to get a good job, admission to a university, or a business opportunity.

*Wasta* is widely regarded as a form of corruption, because intermediaries may require payments for their services. Yet it can be exercised responsibly, as can nepotism and cronyism. The intermediaries can be agents through which a responsible authority figure exercises influence. *Wasta* can also take the form of an administrative service that handles procedures and documents, much as might be done by a lawyer or customs agent. *Wasta* becomes corrupting when intermediaries are motivated by bribes rather than loyalty to a responsible leader. ▪

---

## CASE 7.7

# Gifts to Korean Officials

### SYNOPSIS[12]

While setting up operations in South Korea, a U.S. accounting firm found it necessary to obtain a number of permits from the government. When the approval process bogged down, a local consultant offered to take care of the problem. When asked how, he confided that he would hand his government contact a white envelope—with money inside. His consulting fee would include an unitemized allowance for the payment.

### ANALYSIS

Side payments of this kind are common in Korea, even if large payments are occasionally exposed and bring criminal prosecution. To some extent they result from a blurring of the boundary between gifts and bribes. Businessmen who are granted a meeting with an important official may bring a gift as a token of gratitude, and the gift often takes the form of cash. Gifts of gratitude are culturally appropriate and are not bribes, but if the giver requests a favor, they can slip into the category of bribery. Or a firm might send an official a generous gift in observance of a wedding, or condolence gift in case of death in the family. If the firm subsequently requests a dispensation from the official, the gift looks like a bribe.

Gifts play a functional role by signaling a willingness to cooperate with government officials. Government regulation has played a major part in the remarkable expansion of the Korean economy since the 1960s, particularly where the *chaebol* (large family-run conglomerates) are concerned. In a strongly relationship-based culture like the Korean one, it is unrealistic to try to influence behavior simply by laying down regulations as one might do in Germany or Sweden. A more successful strategy is to implement regulation through personal relationships between businesspeople and government officials. These relationships are established in part by gifts that signal the intent to do what the official wants in exchange for cooperation and favors from the government.

Due to the instability of a purely quid pro quo relationship, it is important not to let gifts slide into obvious bribery. Gifts may also violate such laws as the U.S. Foreign Corrupt Practices Act, which forbids bribery of foreign government officials, even when the payment is made by a local agent (South Korea has a similar law). Because laws of this kind may permit facilitating payments and extortion payments, one should consult an attorney to sort things out. Yet whatever the legal situation, a suitable side payment in the Korean situation is culturally distinguishable from an outright bribe and can pass the generalization test. ▪

---

## CASE 7.8

# Dilemma in Côte d'Ivoire

### SYNOPSIS[13]

"Bending low to enter the small mud hut, I saw her vacant eyes pleading with me to help her. Her name was Josephine Bahonon Ouie, and she was lying on the dirt floor of her mud hut, too sick to move. The true extent of her illness was made obvious by her emaciated body and the bedpan lying next to her. Josephine was one of the 28 women contracted by the government to clean the city.

During my first year as a small business development advisor, I worked with them to form a cooperative group to bypass the lucrative earnings of the middleman and secure higher wages. Although this step was accomplished with relative ease, negotiating on their behalf for better working conditions and regular pay proved difficult, since corruption within the government limited the resources that actually trickled down to the people. Wages were disbursed three months behind schedule, and partial payments were quite common.

"According to her sister, the doctor demanded 16,000 CFA (23 USD) for Josephine's treatment. [The CFA Franc, where CFA stands for Communaute Financiere Africaine, is the currency of 14 African countries.] Because her salary was already three months late, Josephine had obtained credit to pay for her children's school fees, rent for her small hut, and food. She was consequently denied additional credit and could not pay the doctor's fees. As her eyes begged me to help her, Josephine's sister asked me to lend her the money, to be returned once the government paid her wages. As an individual the answer seemed simple; I should lend Josephine the money. She was one of the hardest workers in the cooperative and desperately needed medical attention. However, as a development worker trying to establish a sustainable business project with these women, the answer was not so clear. As in the case of lending funds to a colleague or employee, I would be showing favoritism and erode the common bond among the members of the cooperative. In addition, the gesture would cause the women to view me as a source of funding instead of legitimately working with me to develop projects to address their concerns and issues.

"With these reservations in mind, I sought a solution that would permit me to help Josephine without negatively affecting my role in their cooperative. My first stop was at the Treasury Department. I explained the situation and asked if there was anything that I could do to facilitate the woman's payment. Since this was not the first time that I had confronted them about their tardiness, I knew that one month's salary would be disbursed by the end of the following week. Although not sufficient to pay for all of her treatment, I realized and accepted the extent and limitations of my power within the city government. I quickly moved on to my second stop, the doctor's office. I wanted to know how serious Josephine's condition was and what the treatment would entail. Upon seeing my white skin, the doctor doubled Josephine's medical costs. When I enquired as to what she was suffering from, the doctor replied that it was a combination of typhoid fever, dysentery, and cholera. Further questions and a quick glance through the doctor's medical textbook revealed his rather sketchy understanding of those diseases. I left his office feeling despondent about the quality of medical care in the Ivory Coast but determined to help Josephine.

"I read through several medical books and based on her symptoms, I determined that she was not suffering from typhoid fever or dysentery. Although I did not know her actual illness, I knew she needed to take rehydration salts to regain the water that she had lost due to her illness. I spent the next couple of hours showing her family how to prepare the rehydration salts and insisted that everyone that came in contact with her should wash their hands to prevent the spread of the disease. By the end of the week, she hadn't shown any improvement, and I still hadn't decided how to best handle the situation. Unfortunately, due to political instability I was evacuated from the country. I often wonder about Josephine, is she alive or is she dead? And I wish now that I had just given her the $46.

"Should I have done so?"

## ANALYSIS

This aid worker is concerned that (a) this kind of assistance may create dependency, and (b) it is unfair to help one person when you can't help everyone in need. Argument (a) is a straightforward utilitarian argument, because creating dependency apparently defeats the goal this NGO is trying to achieve in Côte d'Ivoire. Let's deal with argument (b) first, however.

The argument may appear to be a generalization argument, because it says that it is wrong to help one person when you can't generalize the assistance to everyone. But this isn't the generalization test. The test asks whether it is possible for every aid worker in this position to help one person (or more accurately, whether this is consistent with the rationale for the action). This is a very different test, and it's not obvious why the action fails it.

The issue here is not so much generalizability as the more elementary idea that one's own conduct should be consistent: If the circumstances justify aid in one case, then they justify aid in all similar cases. Then what does one do? If many women are equally needy and one cannot help them all, what is the "fair" way to decide who gets help?

This is an interesting puzzle for Western ethics, because apparently the only rational solution is to do nothing and let the woman suffer. Westerners sometimes resolve such dilemmas by drawing lots or whatever, which may satisfy people as "fair" but seems equally irrational.

However, many cultures (including many African cultures) place less emphasis on being "fair" and "rational" in this sense. In practice, one helps when one can and stops helping when one no longer can. There is a strong community ethic in which one is expected to share resources when capable of doing so, and one is equally expected to request help when it is needed. While the West sees this as "dependency," many African cultures see it as a sensible distribution of resources. As Case 7.4 notes, leaders in particular are expected to be generous.

It is hard to draw conclusions for this particular case because there are some 60 cultures in Côte d'Ivoire alone, and all cultures are different. But many African cultures would expect the aid worker to take a leadership position (because he/she is relatively wealthy), give help judiciously when it is possible and needed, and stop giving help when it is no longer possible. Westerners are often reluctant to assume this kind of responsibility, preferring to go by the rulebook rather than make decisions case by case. But in many cultures it is part of the burden of leadership.

Argument (a), the utilitarian argument, must likewise be adjusted to the cultural circumstances. "Dependency" that is dysfunctional in a Western culture reflects a system of redistribution that is quite functional in many traditional cultures. It kept the human species alive for a few hundred thousand years.

Aid agencies commonly warn that preferential treatment will create envy among those who are less favored. This is a Western interpretation of a fundamental trait of many African cultures. When the community comes first and the individual second, standing out above one's fellows (unless one occupies a leadership position and lives up to its obligations) is strongly frowned upon. A competitive economic system, for example, is foreign to these cultures. However, providing assistance to those in need is consistent with this ethic, and in fact required by it because it has a leveling effect. It is therefore important to provide assistance in a way that people see as judicious and conducive to equality rather than inequality. This is consistent with the generalization principle stated at the beginning of this chapter, because it harmonizes with the traditional culture.

This kind of arbitration requires more cultural knowledge than most Westerners have. A possible alternative in such cases is to ask advice from an experienced and trusted person who plays a leadership role in the local community. ■

## ETHICS AND HUMAN NATURE

The normative systems illustrated in these case studies can be seen as growing out of conceptions of human nature. It is a principle reflected in the third condition of rational choice: how we act must reflect who we are.

In a Confucian culture, personhood is defined primarily by relationships with others, particularly the extended family, rather than existence as an individual. It is natural for one member of the family to care for another, as one part of the body cares for another part. Any broader obligation must be grounded in cultivated relationships, whence the importance of *guānxì* and cronyism.

Many African and other traditional cultures locate the basic unit of human existence in the community. Ideally, people do not distinguish their individual welfare from the collective welfare, and the economy is based on sharing of resources. Sharing can occur spontaneously, but the village may benefit from pooling resources and redistributing them according to the wise judgment of a chief.

The Hindu/Buddhist worldview emphasizes connectivity and, in its most rarified expression, interprets human beings as manifestations of a single consciousness (*atman*). This is reflected in a social system that relies fundamentally on connectedness, although the ideal is very imperfectly realized, because only certain kinds of connections matter. Yet civilizations can work gradually toward realization of their ideals, as the West has attempted to do in the area of human rights over the last few centuries.

The Middle East is the birthplace of monotheism, which understands human beings to be creatures of a transcendent God. Because there is a single godhead, his will is the sole standard of behavior. This introduces the idea of universal values, which led to the development of an ethical and legal tradition that strongly influenced the West.

A theme that runs through many of these normative systems is that human beings are linked by a communal conceptual of human nature. People care for each other because they are, in some sense, parts of the same being. Western individualism presents a challenge because it sees human beings as autonomous individuals. Its solution, elaborated throughout this book, is to find unity in reason rather than in ontology. Human beings care for each other because we are rational creatures who must act according to the universal canons of reason. A choice for one is a choice for all and therefore must give everyone equal consideration.

This places a heavy burden on rationality, particularly when religious concepts are not a significant part of public discourse. Rationality has its weak points, as witnessed, for example, by the difficulty of reconciling approaches to distributive justice. Yet it is the way we do it in the West, and we must make it work.

Cultures evolve. Western civilization may at some point modify its reliance on rational individualism, and the rational science and technology that support it, perhaps by incorporating a communal interpretation of personhood. This may be necessary for our survival on a small planet. Yet we are not likely to move to a more adequate worldview until we exhaust the resources of the present one. When we bring to ethics the level of sophistication we bring to science and technology, we will be ready for the next stage.

## Notes

1. The discussion of the case studies (except the last) is based on J. N. Hooker, "Corruption from a cross-cultural perspective," *Cross-Cultural Management: An International Journal*, 16, 2009, pp. 251–267.
2. C. Haberman, "NYC; The ways of taking responsibility," *New York Times*, July 26, 1996.
3. My thanks to Don Lamb, who experienced this scenario and told me the story.
4. For example, Gopinath Munde, *Report to Cabinet Subcommittee to Review the Dabhol Power Project*, 1995.
5. Enron's bribe apparently took the form of a lucrative job offer to Dhar in public relations if he would support Enron's activities (BBC News, "Indian journalist alleges Enron bribe," April 17, 2002).
6. Based on the case study *Lee Kum Kee Co. Ltd. (A): The Family Recipe* by C. Lief and J. L. Ward, Case No. IMD-3-1617, Lausanne: IMD International, 2005.

7. E. Mathieu and S. Freeman, "Three ex-Nortel executives charged," *Toronto Star*, June 19, 2008.
8. Based on the case study *Terry Rhodes* by A. T. Karim, T. Putimahtama, and J. Mullins, London Business School Case No. 708-042-1, 2008.
9. The case description states that certain information, including the location of the events, is disguised. Presumably Guinea is not the real location of the case.
10. This case was provided by an MBA student.
11. F. Adaman, A. Çarkoğlu, and B. Şenatalar, "Corruption in Turkey: Results of a diagnostic household survey," February 2001, http://econ.boun.edu.tr/staff/adaman/research/Corruption.pdf.
12. The late Thomas M. Kerr related this case to me.
13. This case was provided by an MBA student. The student's description of the case is quoted verbatim.

# INDEX